WITHDRAWN

At 33

At 33

Photo by Petersen

At 33

by Eva Le Gallienne

LONGMANS, GREEN AND CO.
NEW YORK · TORONTO
1934

LE GALLIENNE
AT 33

First Edition January 1934
Reprinted four times January 1934
Reprinted March 1934, August 1934
December 1934

To
MY MOTHER

LIST OF ILLUSTRATIONS

At 33

I

Aт seven o'clock on the morning of January eleventh, 1899, in London, England, to the sound of Bow Bells ringing, a cockney baby was brought into the world ; for no baby born within sound of Bow Bells can be anything but cockney. Screaming lustily and unusually hideous, it was a great disappointment to its artistic parents. This was the beginning of my first year. Of course like most human beings I cannot confess to any vivid recollections of this first year of my life. Anything that you will read in this chapter is of necessity written from hearsay. I know that I was exceptionally healthy, exceptionally large, and exceptionally ugly. I grew mightily throughout the year, nursed by Danish lullabies and probably within sound of my father's musical voice reading his latest sonnet. Although I am a cockney by environment of birth, my mother, Julie Norregaard, is pure Danish, and my father though born in England, of Breton descent via the Channel Isles. The important members of my immediate surroundings, besides Father and Mother, were my half-sister Hesper then five years old and, after I reached the great age of six weeks, my Nanny, Susan Stenning, who figures conspicuously in the first ten years

of my life. That is to say in an active way, for in my
memory she will always be a figure of the utmost importance, imbued with a deep tenderness.

Nanny often told me in later years how when Mother
engaged her, she warned her that I was a very ugly child.
Nanny took one look at me and with a burst of affection
that lasted until her death, she exclaimed rapturously,
"But, Madam, she is a *beautiful* baby," and from that
moment on, Nanny loved me with a love that only child-
less women who are born mothers can give.

Another important figure brought into my life by
Nanny in this year was my first doll, Bessie. When
Nanny bought her she had a beautiful china face that
unfortunately I can never claim to have known, for the
first moment she was given me, I flung her from the
perambulator, and smashed her blond Anglo-Saxon
beauty to smithereens leaving a stuffed pink and white
calico body, with strange black stockings, which Nanny
preserved carefully. She made Bessie a face of calico, far
more beautiful I am sure than any porcelain could have
been, with features of india ink and black india ink curls
adorning the forehead. This is the face of the Bessie
that I remember, a Bessie of many faces, for whenever
one grew dirty, Nanny would make another, each one
more beautiful than the one before. At the end of ten
years Bessie must have had as many as twenty-five faces
superimposed one on the other. By that time she must
have been a strange object, but to me she was a real person and was the only doll I ever have loved.

I have vague memories of the Old Manor at Chiddingfold ; Father had discovered it on one of his many bicy-
cling tours.   The prim Georgian façade covered with
neatly trimmed ivy gave no hint of the Elizabethan
luxuriance just behind its back.   But if you crept
through the rhododendron hedge at the side of the front
garden, you suddenly found yourself face to face with a
riot of gables and lattice windows, and left the Georges
far behind.   The old part of the house was covered with
a mass of yellow tea-roses ; it faced a wonderful lawn on
which grew venerable trees, and the garden was gay with
herbaceous borders and rose-paths.

Of course Father, being a poet, had crept through the
rhododendron hedge and had completely fallen under
the spell of this magical place.   It was a fitting home for
a poet, and there he would live !

My first Christmas, my sister tells me, was spent there,
but my recollections of Chiddingfold date from my third
Christmas.   I vaguely remember seeing snow for the first
time ; Nanny helped me make a cake out of it and the
cook put it in the oven where, to my amazement, it
calmly disappeared : witchcraft surely !   Here my memory of Auntie Sissie, Father's sister, hazily takes form, and
that of her husband, James Welch, who was a famous
actor : Uncle Jim we called him.

In the spring of 1902 we left the Old Manor.   The
William Favershams, great friends of Mother's, took it
over, and we moved to London.

We lived in a house in St. John's Wood ; here my

memory begins to take definite shape. The house
seemed enormous to me. Some rooms I remember viv-
idly. It was probably one of the many hundred similar
London houses in the St. John's Wood area : four stories ; the top floor servants' quarters ; at the back a little
garden. The room I remember best was our nursery,
Hesper's and mine. It was on the ground floor with
doors out to the garden. I remember I had a little
wicker arm-chair, a child's chair, that was a great joy to
me. Hep, as I called her (not being able to say Hesper,
but only Hepser, which finally became Hep and always
remained that as far as she and I are concerned), had
wonderful games there. Hep was always wonderful to
me ; gentle, sweet, full of self-abnegation. She inherited
from her Irish mother a fey quality that made her a
curiously magical child. She was so beautiful to look
at, very pale with dark hair, a perfect oval face, and enormous violet eyes like strange flowers. Nanny and her
relatives, all country people, who later will play an important part in this tale, were always afraid she would die
young. They said she was too good and too beautiful to
stay away from God.

I remember the drawing-room. To me, it seemed
very vast. I suppose it was a large room. I know it
had two fireplaces. It was a beautiful room, as are all
rooms my mother has ever made. I carry with me an
impression of old furniture, soft colors, and beautifully
arranged flowers. The drawing-room was an adventure.
I never lived there. I was escorted there, wearing my

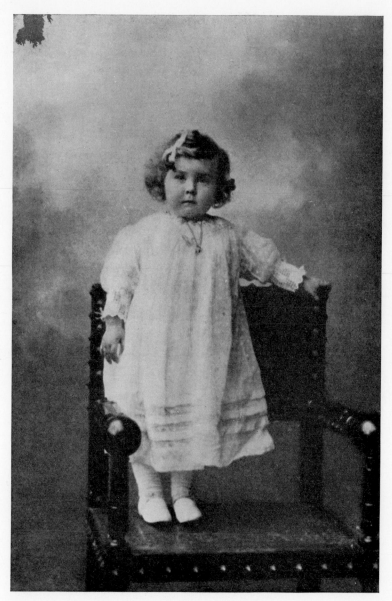

At 2

The Old Manor, Chiddingfold

best bow and my best white dress with insertion in it, that my Danish grandmother had made with her own hands. In the drawing-room I always felt very important and a little strange. Usually there were a lot of grown-ups there, important and interesting people, as I afterwards discovered ; mostly artists, writers, painters, musicians, but at that time just "grown-ups" who treated me with a certain over-elaborate kindness and attention that somehow offended me. My impression is of people attractive, well groomed, who smelt nice and as a rule had well-modulated voices, a thing to which I have always been very sensitive. The strongest memory I have of my father at this period is his voice, which even at this early age affected me as a thing of great beauty.

I remember our night nursery. A vivid scene : I had been especially naughty. I can see Hep's unhappy face. Nanny was giving me the severest punishment. I was so naughty that she was going away. She couldn't stay another moment with such a bad little girl. She packed her bag, put on the blue cloak of her nurse's uniform, the little straw bonnet with blue ribbons that nurses wore at that period, and left the room and presumably the house, for good. An impression of utter agony. Nanny had gone. She had deserted me. I would never see her again. Screaming and yelling, in nightgown and bare feet, I rushed out to look for her all over the house. After I had yelled myself into complete repentance Nanny appeared from behind a door where she had been hiding, and with loud cries of "I will never do it again,"

I persuaded her to unpack and remain with us. Where-upon I cried myself to sleep and decided to be virtuous and good from then on. This episode, it is needless to say, was often repeated right up to the time when Nanny left me many years later.

I remember my mother's bedroom. This was the scene of my first violent assertion that the Theatre was to be my life. In the afternoon I had been taken to see "The Water Babies," my first play. Mother was dress-ing to go to a dinner party. I proved difficult in the night nursery and insisted on being taken to see Mother. I entered in wild hysterics, screaming at the top of my lungs that I wanted to be a water baby, that I must be a water baby, that I *would* be a water baby. Mother was almost late for her dinner party. She was charming but adamant. She said she would be glad to take me to the manager of the theatre and tell him I insisted on being a water baby, but that the first question he would ask me was whether I could read or write. This, with the unfortunate logic of mind that I have always had, seemed to me an insuperable obstacle. Immediately I became calm and resigned but imbued with an indomitable re-solve that read and write I would and that a water baby I therefore would become.

In this seemingly calm state of resignation, through momentary necessity, I was hauled to bed by Nanny and went grimly to sleep. Mother arrived at her dinner party just in time.

HEP and I were sent with Nanny to her old home in Farncombe for Christmas. Nanny belonged to a family of nine : two boys and seven girls. Her people had for generations lived in Farncombe in the same cottage, and had run the forge there. The Stennings' cottage was a landmark in the little village. Since the house had been built it had been inhabited by her ancestors, all important people in the little community. Her father, whom I remember as a sweet old man with quite a long beard, had been blacksmith there for years, head of his own forge and that of his father and grandfather and great-grandfather before him. He had been elected mayor of the town but, being a modest and retiring sort of man, had refused to undertake this responsibility. His two sons died, and through some curious old law of England, the property, therefore, eventually passed out of the jurisdiction of his daughters ; but when we knew them first they were still ensconced in this extraordinary old house.

It was a very early Elizabethan cottage, almost entirely supported by an enormous ivy tree, that one could not encompass with two hands, which seemed to hold in its evergreen claws the old house in a firm grip that withstood the years. The rooms were so low that I remember my sister Hesper, when she was twelve years old, trying to practise the violin in the living-room and not being able to, for on the upper strokes her bow touched the ceiling. It was a divine old house. *Oak, oak, oak !*

Lattice windows mullioned. *Ivy, ivy, ivy!* supporting everything. Old staircases ; recesses ; old floors, bent, worn with age ; delightful old corners and cupboards and passages, to a child so full of mystery and excitement ; and at the back an old, old garden filled with apple-trees and flanked by a hedge of hop-vines, that grew so high they seemed illimitable ; a garden full of mystery and wonder, peopled now in our memories (Hep's and mine) with ghosts and fairies that enriched our childhood with terror and magic. Only people who have known old English gardens can understand what an old English garden can mean.

At this time there were living there Nanny's father, old Mr. Stenning, and her sisters Sarah, Annie, and Julia Rosa, whom we always called "Juden." Mr. Stenning, whom I remember as a very old man, much respected and venerated, did little but potter about the garden smoking his pipe and also occupying the best room in the house. In true English fashion he, being the only surviving male of the family line, was pampered and given in to on every count. He was the head of the household. Juden's best rice pudding gave up its choicest morsel to him, as well as her roast beef, pork, the first fruits of the garden, and all the most succulent dishes that she, as one of the best cooks that I have ever known in my life, could concoct. This was all very right and very proper according to the old English tradition, and I must say that dear old Mr. Stenning deserved it all.

Sarah (always called "Sy") was the gardener, and also

Bessie
At 5 with Nanny

At 6
At 8

The Old Forge, Farncombe, Surrey
Tea in the Garden — from left to right: Eva, Juden, Anne, Nanny, Hep

the politician of the family. She had been chamber-
maid for several years to Lord and Lady Something-or-
other and had gained vast cosmopolitan experience
through trips to "Dinard" and "Dinang," to which she
always referred when it came to a point of settling difficult and world-wide political matters. As a matter of
fact she showed far greater sense than a lot of people
whose experience encompassed a wider range ; and her
flowers and vegetables were beyond compare !

Annie took care of the house. She was always teased
by the rest of the family for being "High-Church." She
was very aristocratic in her tendencies and evolved by
herself an entirely new French language, under Hep's
and my influence, that only Hep and I could possibly
understand.

Juden, the youngest of the family, was the cook. Unlike most English cooks she was extraordinarily good.
In fact in all my life I never remember eating such good
food as Juden made. She was very shy, very retiring,
very humble, and most human in understanding. If
one were ever punished for no matter what fault, Juden
would always be there to defend one and give a piece of
treacle pie to the penitent exiled to the scullery. Juden
was the great consoler. Since Nanny's death she is the
one who has inherited her looks and her tenderness ;
children love her. That was always the secret of Nanny's magic : children loved her and therefore respected
her and obeyed her.

The Christmas of 1903 Hep and I spent in Farn-

combe.   Troubles we knew nothing of were going on in
London.   We were happy.   We played in the snow in
the old garden.   We ran our hoops through the snow
and ice in the country lanes, and on Christmas day we
had our tree in the living-room of the old cottage.   At
the top of the tree was our usual Christmas angel — a
Danish angel of wax with tinsel wings and a star in her
flaxen hair ; on the lower branches many presents of a
modest kind, provided mostly by Mrs. Norris, the baker
of Farncombe ; and on one of the uppermost branches,
a golliwog with jet black face and calico eyes for me.
He stayed with me for many years, though my devotion
to Bessie remained paramount.

I remember a sudden change.   Everything seemed
queer.   Hep and I loved Farncombe.   We had been
happy with Nanny, Sy, Annie and Juden.   Young children so easily accustom themselves in a few weeks to an
environment that, finding ourselves suddenly thrust out
of it, we imagined we should never be there again.   Hep
was to go to Aunt Sissie and Uncle Jim ; Nanny and I
were to join Mother in Paris.

We started.   Nanny was one of those incorrigibly
British Englishwomen with certain very definite standards.   You could not cross the Channel without being
seasick.   Nothing outside of England was any good.
Salad must not be eaten, nor any of the new-fangled
food provided on the Continent.   If Nanny bought me
a toy she would always look to see if it had "Made in
England" on it, otherwise she would not spend any

money on it, for it would "fall to pieces in a moment."
She was (God bless her) the most insular type of Englishwoman that ever set forth, of course with misgivings,
from the shores of the British Isles.

We arrived at the boat at Newhaven and went into
our second-class cabin ; Nanny at once saying that we
had to lie down for she already felt deathly sick. I, of
Viking birth, having never been sick in my life, nor
my parents before me, was reluctantly forced to lie down
on my back accompanied by my faithful Bessie, surrounded by British ladies of the lower bourgeoisie, all
intent on being violently ill at once according to true
British tradition. I surmounted this hypnotic urge to
seasickness, and being young enough went fast asleep and
woke to real consciousness only when we arrived in Paris.

Here I was driven with Nanny through a barrage of
incomprehensible language to a small hotel in the rue
Vaugirard, where Mother met us walking down a beautiful flight of stairs in her usual beautiful manner.

The next thing that I remember clearly is that we lived
in an apartment at 60 rue Vaugirard. It was a very old
house which had probably, in times gone by, been a private residence of some distinction. We lived on the fifth
floor and of course there was no such thing as an elevator.
But Mother made the place delightful. It was rather
low-ceilinged but quite spacious according to our American point of view. I think there were about six rooms.
The floors were made of hexagonal tiles of red brick
worn with age ; even at that time they gave me great

satisfaction, and I often wish now that people would make floors like this. A large room on the courtyard served as both kitchen and dining-room.

I was so young at this time that I was not conscious of the exact situation in which we found ourselves. It was only much later that I discovered the true heroism of both my Mother and Nanny. Mother, having found life with my father no longer possible, had decided to leave him and live on her own. Money was extremely scarce. She managed to eke out a very frugal living by translating from the Nordic languages and by a little newspaper work. Nanny, who, when Mother engaged her, had many pretensions in the way of demanding a nurse-maid and various extras that prevented her from stooping to any menial labor, presently realized Mother's need and, having become profoundly attached to both of us, decided to cast in her lot with ours. As Mother afterwards told me, she worked for us for over a year without any pay ; worked in a way that she would previously have considered beneath her. In short she scrubbed, cleaned, did the washing, cooked, and looked after us entirely. I know that Mother has never forgotten this wonderful and loyal devotion.

From now on and for the next eight years the Luxembourg Gardens became a great factor in my life. Every day Nanny took me there for several hours in the afternoon. She soon discovered, with her never-failing British flair, an old Englishwoman, probably the only one in Paris to keep one of the little candy booths of which

there are several in the Gardens. This was Madame
Kapelaer, who in 1870 had come from England and
married a Frenchman employed in one of the many thousand civic offices of France. Like all members of the
French bureaucracy, he enjoyed the privilege of leaving
his wife pensioned, and in this particular case her pen-
sion rights assigned her this booth in the Luxembourg
Gardens. There she sat, from ten in the morning till
the Gardens closed, dispensing all kinds of maliciously
flavored soda-waters, sugar-sticks, chocolate-creams, and
long strips of licorice that we used to call *caoutchouc*.
(Their name was extremely relevant, for they indeed resembled rubber bands !) Madame Kapelaer, for all the
years I was in Paris, was a vastly important figure to me
and the whole young Anglo-American colony. At this
particular time she practically saved Nanny's life. Darling Nanny, who was so homesick for England, the English language (her French was always completely and extraordinarily lacking), English food — in short, for the
British vibration.

At this time I was taken to my first kindergarten. I
remember that it was on the rue Bonaparte near the
Place Saint Sulpice.

We were taught to read by a curious phonetic method
that also involved a series of Delsartian signs, at that
time considered a great innovation. I suppose it was all
right, for I did manage to learn to read, though I was
quite slow at it ; but I remember Nanny informing
Mother one day in a state of fury that the concierge,

who had seen me practising my A B C at the dining-room window, had asked with great interest whether I was deaf and dumb. My greatest amusement at this time was to play in the yard with the concierge's daughter who was about my age (of course this was after Nanny had hotly denied my deaf-and-dumbness). They had a parrot called Jacquot, as all French parrots are called, who became my great friend. The concierge was very ambitious to have Jacquot learn some English. His vocabulary consisted of the only English words French people ever know : "How-do-you-do, bifstake, plum-pudding, water-closet." This interesting collection I increased with "hello," "how are you," and "pretty Polly."

It was during this time that the Melziners came to see us. Leo and Joe, both well known now in the theatre world of America, were at that time the only children that I knew. Mr. Melziner had a studio off the Boulevard Montparnasse, and I remember one exciting visit when Leo (now Kenneth McKenna) showed me his toy train electrically run, which I thought was the most thrilling thing I had ever seen in my life. I think it was the first time I ever envied anyone anything and incidentally, also, one of the last. I remember Joe very well. I think he was about a year younger than I. He was a pink-faced little rogue of a boy and I liked him very much.

In the same apartment house lived an English writer, Miss Hallard, with whom Mother became friendly. They collaborated for a while on the translation of a very

difficult book.   Miss Hallard quickly won my respect and
affection through her possession of six tortoises, gradu-
ated in size, all beautiful and impeccably trained.

Every day at noon — at *midi,* that is — they sat
solemnly in a row and received, starting with the largest,
a beautiful lettuce leaf.   I considered it an enormous
privilege to see this ceremony.   Several times a week
Miss Hallard would take them in a basket to the Luxembourg, and would sit on a bench, reading or working,
while the tortoises in a tandem-harness made of ribbons
would enjoy themselves in the grass.   These constitute
my major recollections of the rue Vaugirard, in which I
think we lived over a year.

The next change I remember was moving to the rue
de Regard.   This was a most exciting change, for Hep
and Auntie Sissie were to come and live with us.   I loved
them both and looked forward especially to having Hep
again.

This apartment was larger and it seemed to me much
grander than the one at rue Vaugirard.   Hep and I had
a nursery together looking out over the courtyard.   Next
door was Mother's bedroom ; then there was what
seemed to me then an enormous dining-room.   There
was also a drawing-room, spacious too, which I only remember vaguely, and Auntie Sissie's room ; besides
which Nanny had her own sleeping quarters.

On the opposite side of the street was an old convent-
school to which Hep and I were sent.   The teachers
were all unfrocked nuns who carried on, in their

spirit and behavior, the tradition of the convent. Hep
and I were the only Protestants in the school. We were
looked upon as something alien, but at the same time
interesting as furnishing a variation in the routine. We
were absolved from the weekly confession, and on the
daily walk to Saint Sulpice we were given special permission not to kiss Saint Peter's toe or to make a genuflec-
tion at the altar. I still remember the sewing class, in
which I never progressed farther than hemming, while
all the other girls made miraculous buttonholes and
broderie Anglaise to the accompaniment of the "Hail
Marys" which were a regular part of the sewing
hour.

The hours at this school were quite long. We went
there at eight o'clock, had lunch there, and must have
been there until dinner-time, for I remember at four
o'clock being let out into the yard for *goûter,* which consisted of a roll and a tablet of chocolate. This was a
turbulent and noisy performance. We screamed and
yelled for half an hour and then went back again for
more work until about six.

I have one vivid recollection of a Ste. Catherine *fête.*
There were to be magic-lantern slides among other entertainments. I had been naughty, I can't remember about
what, and as a punishment was forbidden to see the
magic-lantern. Hep, who was always my champion and
defender, was so incensed that she braved all the teachers, even the headmistress, and made such a scene and
cried and screamed so loudly that the performance could

not begin in peace until I had been rescued from an up-
stairs class-room and admitted to the show. That same
day there was a further entertainment that to Hep and
me seemed utter barbarism and against which we rose in
revolt. This was a game which consisted in enclosing a
live rabbit in an earthenware pot suspended from the ceiling. Each girl in turn was allowed to strike at this pot
with a wooden mallet, and the one who broke it and released the animal won a prize. Hep and I had no idea
of what it was all about until we caught sight of the poor
terrified rabbit flying for safety, but already so bruised
and frightened that it could scarcely breathe. We had
a fearful row with everybody and left in horror, for we
had always loved animals so much, and treated them with
the respect due their dignity.

About this time I remember one eventful Easter Sunday when the famous writer Arnold Bennett had invited
Mother to visit him at Fontainebleau for the day and
drive in his new motor-car. Nanny, Hep, Bessie, and I
were included in the invitation.

There was great excitement. Only Nanny had serious objections ; she had no patience with these new-
fangled inventions — "nasty, smelly things" that covered
you with dust if you happened to be going for a peaceful
walk along a country road. And anyhow, she had serious fears that at the speed they went (fifteen miles an
hour — who ever heard of such a thing !) one would not
be able to catch one's breath. There was sure to be a
dreadful accident !

The motor-car drove up with incredible noise, dust, and smell.

It was shaped like a governess cart (this comforted Nanny a little !) ; Mr. Bennett sat next to the chauffeur on a very high seat like a carriage-box. We clambered into our seats through a little door at the back of the car, and sat there perched very high, in considerable trepidation.

After a great number of terrifying explosions, accompanied by Nanny's outcries of alarm, the motor-car gathered speed and rushed at fifteen miles an hour along the avenues through the forest.

At first I remember being rather afraid of Mr. Bennett. He had a walrus-moustache that made a great impression on me. He won me finally by presenting me with a bag full of chocolate-cream eggs which I decidedly appreciated.

The ride came to an end without undue mishap ; on the way home to the rue de Regard Nanny confided that if the "nasty things" had to be, she preferred *riding* in them to being covered with dust standing by the roadside ; as a matter of fact she had enjoyed herself immensely !

The only animals we had at this time were birds. My little Danish grandmother — Bet, as we called her, from the Danish *Bestemoder* — had come on a visit to Paris and had presented me with about twelve little tropical birds in a big cage. She made with her own hands a green cloth coverlet with *Eva* embroidered in the corner,

with which to cover them at night.   They were our great
pride.

I must confess that my true love at that time, in spite
of my admiration for these beautiful birds, was given to
a common sparrow which, as a weak baby, with scarcely
a feather to his name, I had found in the courtyard and
carefully carried to my room where for days I fed it on
sugar and water, keeping it in an overturned paper-basket
in which I had arranged a perch.   This sparrow stayed
with me all winter and was so tame that it flew freely
about the room, perching on my head and shoulder and
I am afraid in no way contributing to the cleanliness
which Nanny always insisted on.   Finally one day in
the spring, a warm day, when the leaves were green and
the sun was shining brightly, he flew away, strong, well,
and I think perhaps grateful, to build his own nest and
become head of his own household.

Bessie, my doll, had been with me all these years.   At
this time she must have been wearing her fifteenth face,
which was extraordinarily becoming.   My grandmother
had made her a lovely new dress, and I myself had made
her a blue serge bonnet with a light blue bow, out of
some ribbon from a chocolate box.   Bessie is the chief
protagonist in one of the most tragic scenes of my life in
the rue de Regard.

Mother had some great friends, Mr. and Mrs. Oliver
Bodington.   He was an Englishman, she an American.
They had three sons : George, John, and Nicholas.
George was about Hep's age, perhaps a little older.

John was a couple of years older than I, and Nicholas a couple of years younger. They were giving a children's party. Hep and I were invited. They always had at their parties the most fashionable children from the American colony in Paris, and Mam was most anxious that Hep and I should not shame the family honor. Hep was always easy and amenable, but it was always with great difficulty that Mam, with Nanny's help, could scrub me and polish me and thrust me into my grand party dress, which I disliked intensely.

We started down the stairs. We were to drive in a carriage, which was very exciting. Grasping Bessie by the hand, feeling stiff and uncomfortable in my grand dress, with Mam's words ringing in my ears, "Now do try to be sweet, 'Nutie'; speak up when you are spoken to," I solemnly went towards the cab. At this moment Nanny, who was smartly dressed in her best nurse's uniform of black alpaca, with stiff white collar and cuffs, her navy blue cape and bonnet with ribbons freshly ironed, caught sight of Bessie. "What have you got there?" she said. "What is this nonsense, taking that old Bessie with you? What would Mam say? What will all the little girls say when they see you with that dirty old thing?"

"But, Nanny, I want to take Bessie with me. I love my Bessie. I want her to come to the party," I said with tears of anger at the insult and anguish at the thought of going without her, in my voice.

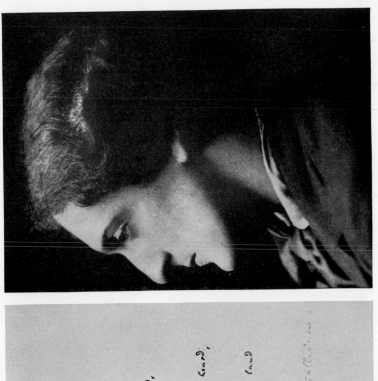

Ah ! did you ever hear the spring
calling you through the snow,
Or hear the little blackbird sing
Inside its egg — or go
To that green land where grass begins,
Each tiny seed, to grow ?

O have you heard what some has heard,
Or seen what some has seen ;
O have you been to that strange land
Where no one else has been !

Richard Le Gallienne.

My mother

"Stop that nonsense and give her to me," said Nanny. "Little ladies don't behave like that."

Whereupon she seized Bessie and deposited her in the concierge's lodge, while Hep, trying to console me, led me to the cab through my shrieks of "I don't want to be a little lady. I won't be a little lady. I don't want to go without my Bessie!" Scarlet in the face and convulsed with sobs, I arrived at the party, where I sat all afternoon in a corner without saying a word and was roused to activity only by a large dish of ice cream and several pieces of cake, which I devoured in silence, and in a kind of sullen rage. This is the first party I remember clearly. No wonder I have had a distaste for parties ever since.

II

THE next home I remember is No. 1 rue de Fleurus.
We moved there, Mother, Nanny and I ; Auntie Sissie
and Hep went back to England. Mother, who had
always been phenomenally clever with her hands, besides having unerring taste in all matters of dress, had
decided to start a hat shop. During the last months at
the rue de Regard, she had been quietly preparing herself. She wanted to know the business from the bottom
up, so she worked for more than six months as an *ap-
prentie* in the establishment of one of the big French mo-
distes and, having secured a little capital, started work on
her own. She did not want to exploit my father's name,
and decided to run her business under a pseudonym. She
chose the name of "Mme. Fédora." Here the influence
of Bernhardt shows, for Mother had had a great admiration for her since she was a young girl in Copenhagen,
where Mme. Sarah came on one of her world *tournées,*
and she had seen her play in "Fédora" and "Froufrou"
among other things.

Mother started in a modest way with one assistant.
Her clientele was mostly American, and I know of several ladies now who say they have never been able to

find hats to their liking since Mme. Fédora left Paris and
gave up this work for the even harder task of steering
unruly me through my first theatre years.   In the daytime her drawing-room was turned into a salon.   Next
door to it was the little *atelier,* and in the evenings the
hats that had stood proudly on their stands all day were
put away in boxes ; the ribbons, feathers and flowers, the
elaborate garnitures of that period, vanished into unknown hiding places, and from six o'clock onward Mme.
Fédora's *salon de modes* became the drawing-room of
Mrs. Le Gallienne.

Here Mother and I would spend the evening.   I can
see her so clearly, leaning on the railing of the open
French window, smoking her after-dinner cigarette, as I
leaned beside her, and we both looked out over the beautiful chestnut-trees of the Luxembourg Gardens opposite.   We would exchange notes on our day.   She would
tell me of a wonderful hat that was being made for Mrs.
Somebody-or-other, of whether it had been a good day
or a bad.   And I would tell of my adventures at the little
school around the corner in the rue Jean-Bart, run by a
sweet old couple called Duvernois ; then Nanny would
come in and call "Bed-time, my pet lamb," and I would
go off to bed with Bessie clasped tightly in my arms.

Although I was very slow at learning to read, once I
mastered this art, I became a voracious reader.   Mother
put no restrictions of any kind on my books, knowing
well that what I couldn't understand would not interest
me, nor would it harm me.   The first book I read to my-

self, I remember clearly, was "Robinson Crusoe." Then I developed a veritable passion for Dumas : "The Count of Monte Cristo," "The Three Musketeers" and all its sequels. Then came an orgy of Dickens and Thackeray. Mother had read to me many of Andersen's "Fairy Tales," and I also discovered Grimm's goblins and the Andrew Lang books — also the Knights of the Round Table. These I devoured, living an inner life of breathless adventure in which I was all the chief characters in turn. Sometimes I would start off for school as Sir Galahad, sometimes as the Lady Iseult, sometimes as the old witch in "Hänsel and Gretel," (I was certainly versatile in those days !) ; and I think my dear old teacher, Mme. Duvernois, would have been dismayed and astonished had she known of the various fantastic personages that entered her austere class-room, concealed beneath the stolid and robust exterior of *"la petite Éva,"* then aged eight.

That summer we went to England, and a great grief came to my dear mother. Her beloved friend, Sissie Welch, Auntie Sissie, fell ill and died under an operation. Of course, at the age of eight you have no consciousness of death, no understanding of it. It means no more than distance : someone who was there has gone somewhere else — and your sense of time is so retarded that to be told you will *never* see anyone again, or you will not see someone for *a year,* represents about the same degree of woe.

Hep and I were sent to visit Nanny's married sister,

Mrs. Wilson, whose husband was one of the head game-keepers in Epping Forest, and who lived in a lovely old house on the edge of the great woods. It was a beautiful spot full of adventures for children, especially for children whose imaginations bristled with fairies and elves and knights and beautiful princesses. Hep, who was older than I, and who had loved Auntie Sissie dearly, was hard to console, but the austere beauty of the forest, the sunny flower-laden glades, literally carpeted with blossoms, the deer, the rabbits and the birds, soothed and comforted her and we spent happy hours together that summer.

On returning to London many changes awaited us. Hep was to stay on with Uncle Jim — James Welch — and Mother and I were to return to Paris, but this time *without Nanny*. The climate in Paris did not agree with her, and it was found wiser for her to stay on in England and work there. Of course I knew nothing of all this, and it must have been terribly hard for Mother to break it to me. I was told nothing until we were quite ready for the journey. Nanny appeared as usual ; I thought her eyes looked funny ; she kissed me and hugged me a great deal and then went out of the room. Mother brought me a little basket containing an adorable gray and black striped kitten, which of course delighted me, and it was not until we were in the four-wheeler en route for the station that I asked where Nanny was. There was a strange girl there, a maid ;

everything seemed obscure and foreboding and mixed
up. I was told : then the deluge ! Poor Mother ! It
must have been a difficult journey for her.

I have always felt that my grown-up days began with
Nanny's departure. I had somehow never visualized a
life without my Nanny, and I felt strange and quite old.
It was my first real grief.

In Paris were more changes. I was to be sent to a
grown-up school. A very important, serious school.
Mother had chosen carefully and she chose well : the
Collège Sévigné.

This school was at No. 8 rue de Condé — it was situated in the old Hôtel de Condé, a palace famous in history. The class-rooms were large, with immensely high
ceilings and tall narrow French windows, beautiful *boise-
ries,* parquet floors and wonderful carved mantelpieces.
One seemed to see the ghosts of bygone days roaming
about the halls, and hear the clattering of phantom horses
on the cobblestones of the courtyard. For about fifty
years it had been used as a school, and the children had
not treated it with due respect ! There was an atmosphere of French ink about the place (it has a pungent
smell different from all other inks) and there were ink
stains on the gray paneled walls and on the noble floors.
The desks were black, of the old-fashioned kind, with
sloping lids that lifted (a great convenience to school
children ; it's too bad that some educator seems to have
found that out !). At the end of the room on a raised

platform were the teacher's desk and the blackboard ;
old maps were on the wall, and busts of Voltaire and
Molière on the chimneypiece.

At the time I joined the school, the headmistress was a
very old woman ; almost a dwarf, she was hunch-backed,
with a keen clever face in which I remember very piercing black eyes.　She was a brilliant scholar ; her name
was Mlle. Salomon.　The school, considered very highly
in Paris, was secular : there was no religious teaching.
It was run like a college and prepared girls for the Sor-
bonne.　Its students took themselves very seriously and
were in a good way to becoming real blue-stockings.
But how they taught there !　The hours were short :
8 to 12 ; but during those hours you had to *work*.　Then
of course there was home work.　The lessons were given
in the form of lectures by distinguished professors, all
specialists in their own fields.　We took notes, and those
who didn't attend were out of luck.　They made you
use your own brains.　I think it is the best form of education imaginable.

Every morning I would start off with my student's
serviette under my arm and feeling enormously important would walk through the Luxembourg Gardens to
the gate opposite the Odéon Theatre, walk under its
arcades, cross the Place de l'Odéon and down into the
Rue de Condé to No. 8 where hung the great sign COL-
LÈGE SÉVIGNÉ.　A bell in the courtyard would be clang-
ing a warning that classes would start in five minutes.
In the class-rooms there was the usual turmoil; last-minute

consultations on the correct answer to a problem ; a
glance at someone else's essay in the hope of gleaning
something useful in case one had been lazy ; then the
putting on of black serge pinafores ; the din rising in
volume ; the sudden hush as the professor entered. At
the end of an hour the bell clanged again ; five minutes
to prepare for the next class, until at *midi* the final bell
and release for the day !

I would walk home and have lunch with Mother ; she
would go back to her work as Mme. Fédora, and I would
dash out to the Luxembourg to roller-skate, or sail a boat
on the pond, or eat *caoutchoucs* at Mme. Kapelaer's.
One day as I was launching my boat, bound on some Viking expedition, I heard a small boy, also with a boat,
singing "Yankee Doodle" in a lusty voice. I called out
to him, "Are you English ?" "Of course not ! *American !*" he yelled, in a tone that was meant to put me in
my place but didn't. I immediately began, "Rule,
Britannia" in a loud voice, but was unable to drown his
"Yankee Doodle" with which he immediately retaliated.
In spite of this ominous prelude to our acquaintance we
became great friends. He was the son of the well-known
American painter Augustus Koopman, and he and his
father and mother and his sister Ellen all lived in the
same house as we did in the rue de Fleurus. They were
a source of great joy to me, the Koopmans. We became
almost inseparable. Ellen was sent to the Collège, and
she and I and Bernard and a few other American kids
became the terrors of the Luxembourg guards, for our

favorite game was doing what was forbidden. If there were signs "Do not walk on the grass," we would roll on it, and when a guard came in sight run off screaming like a flock of birds. We climbed the statues, we waded in the fountains, we made fortresses out of the iron chairs for hire ; in other words we were a terrible nuisance and had a marvelous and unforgettable amount of fun.

But what gave me the greatest pleasure of all was the donkey and goat carts that made the tour of the *bassin* loaded with tiny baby passengers, at ten centimes a trip. I was, of course, not interested in riding in the carts ; that would have been beneath my dignity, but I had managed to make friends with the girl who managed the business, and on crowded afternoons, Sundays, and half-holidays, was allowed to take charge of one of the chariots and proudly lead it round through the crowded paths shouting, *"Attention, s'il vous plaît !"* in stentorian tones. I think nothing else in life has ever given me such a sense of importance. The babies had to be hoisted into the carriage and carefully strapped in, for though we went at a snail's pace, the mothers were terrified of an "accident." When all the passengers were securely fastened in their seats, the money had to be collected, and when it had been safely deposited in Thérèse Coudret's leather bag worn at her belt, I stepped to the donkey's head, cracked my whip, and with an *"Attention, s'il vous plaît, nous partons !"* the whole procession started off.

Then came the thrilling moment when, the day's work over, the animals and carts were returned to their stable.

Thérèse Coudret was a daughter of the head gardener of the Luxembourg. They lived in the Orangerie, a part of the garden closed to the public, where the hot-houses and great conservatories were. Next to their house was the little stable, the home of the many fas-cinating donkeys and goats that made up their menagerie. You passed through a gate on which appeared in large letters : *Le public n'entre pas ici !* (that in itself was enough to make you feel like a God !) but once inside you suddenly came across the tiny stable, immaculately neat, so cosy and sweet-smelling, with beds of bright golden straw, on which the milk-white goats, the black goats, and the *café au lait* goat settled themselves com-fortably ; then the donkeys were unharnessed and rubbed down before joining the goats in the golden straw. It was like a *crêche*. The Coudrets, Madame and Thérèse especially, adored their animals, and there was a feeling of peace and contentment in that little colony of beasts.

I never go to Paris without visiting the Coudrets ; it is a sweet wholesome world that has never changed. Thérèse is a little older, so am I, so is Madame, but the *crêche* is still the same ; there is something poignantly touching about the place to me now that brings a lump in my throat. I come away refreshed and full of quiet happiness.

Sometimes on Sundays Mother and I would go off on expeditions : to the Bois de Boulogne ; to Versailles, where we had lunch in a little restaurant at the foot of the *tapis vert ;* and best of all to Ville d'Avray where, beside the pond immortalized in Du Maurier's "Peter Ibbetson," we would take our *déjeuner* at the Hotel Cabassud, and walk back to Neuilly through the woods, returning home by way of the little river steamer on the Seine.

Then came a very special Sunday afternoon when Mother took me to the Théâtre Sarah Bernhardt to see "La Belle au Bois Dormant" (The Sleeping Beauty) in which Mme. Sarah Bernhardt, *La Grande Sarah* as the French always affectionately and reverently called her, was to play the Prince : *le Prince Charmant*.

Mother had taken the tickets a long time ahead and the day was looked forward to with immense excitement. We were to have lunch at Boulant's, a restaurant which is still flourishing on the Boulevard des Italiens, and we sat at a table on the first floor by the window, looking down on the busy Sunday life of the boulevards. After lunch, which I was too excited to enjoy, though as a rule my appetite in those days was gargantuan, we walked down to the rue St. Honoré and turning to the left started towards the Place du Châtelet. I was sure we would be late ! To my horror Mother ran into a friend, a charming Danish woman, Jenny Hagelstam, of whom I was usually very fond, but whom on this particular occasion I devoutly wished elsewhere. They talked on in Danish for what seemed to me an eternity ; we should certainly be late ! I felt a lump coming into my throat, and my eyes began to burn. I pulled at Mother's skirt. She and Mrs. Hagelstam laughed a good deal in what I

thought was an extremely unnecessary and aggravating
way, and at last, after interminable good-byes and more
laughter, Mother took me by the hand and we started
off again, arriving finally at the Place du Châtelet where
the Théâtre Sarah Bernhardt stands impressively on one
side of the square, with the Théâtre du Châtelet facing
it on the other.

Having successfully gone through all the torments of
the *bureau de location,* the program sellers, and the
ouvreuses (old harpies wearing pale blue rosettes in their
hair, who try to wrest your garments from you in order
to place them in the *vestiaire* or cloak-room, from which
they are practically unredeemable) we found ourselves
at last, though to my amazement a full twenty minutes
early, on the first row of the balcony, splendidly situated
very near the stage.

It is a huge old theatre in many tiers, horseshoe-shaped,
all gold and red — just what a theatre should be.   I sat
in awed silence, too excited to speak.   The houselights
dimmed, the footlights went up, the curtain rose on a
prologue in a forest in which many animals, including
frogs with electric eyes, came to life and held some kind
of conference.   Then the scene changed to a room in a
cottage, where a grandmother sat at her spinning-wheel.

A sudden thrill went through the house as a voice
was heard outside the door of the cottage.   Too many
people have tried to describe that voice for me to attempt
it ; such things cannot be put into words.   The old theatre suddenly seemed to vibrate and quiver as though the

magical spirit of life itself had animated its old frame.
The door opened ; a young boy leapt onto the stage, his
arms full of lilacs which he impetuously flung at the feet
of his old grandmother.

This young boy was *La Grande Sarah.*

To attempt to describe what this performance meant
to me would be impossible.   I sat in a trance, unable to
breathe, unable to utter a word, so profoundly moved
and impressed that at the end of the play — which came,
alas, all too soon ! — I could only heave a great sigh of
anguish as Mother led me out, my eyes to the last moment glued to the curtain which I so hoped might go
up again.

It was not until many hours later that I could speak,
and try to tell Mother how I felt.   She has told me since
what an ordeal the performance was to her.   She admired and loved Sarah Bernhardt as the greatest actress
she had ever seen, and knowing her to be over sixty, and
knowing the keen and ruthless critical faculty of a child,
she had been terrified that I might only see an old woman
dressed up as a prince, and that it would seem funny to
me, that I perhaps would scoff.   Darling Mother, she
needn't have worried !   What I saw was the very essence
and spirit of youth, romance and beauty.   From that
moment on, the Theatre, which I had rather discarded
of late in my thoughts, became to me the all-important
aim ; all my experiences, my reading, my studies from
then on were focussed towards one ultimate goal from
which I never again wavered for an instant : the Theatre ;

the power of the Theatre to spread beauty out into life. To be a worker in, a part of such a power seemed to me something worth struggling for.

The years went by. We sometimes went to Copenhagen for Christmas ; there I learned Danish, and became great friends with my cousin Mogens Norregaard, a few months older than I, who is now a well-known painter and lives in Rome (we had wonderful talks about our respective "arts" and dreamt many dreams together). My dear Uncle Kai Norregaard often took me to the Royal Theatre in Copenhagen, that beautiful old theatre with such a fine record, where the words *Ej Blot til Lyst* (Not only for amusement), are carved over the proscenium arch. Above all there was my dear little grandmother Bet, beloved of all the family, who used to read me Hans Christian Andersen in the original Danish, and in her old quavering voice would teach me folksongs and nursery rhymes of Scandinavia.

In Paris Mother worked hard and her business grew in importance until we finally left the rue de Fleurus and took a *"grand"* apartment in the Rue Tronchet just behind the Madeleine. I kept on at the Collège Sévigné, read a great deal, and saw a great many beautiful things in the theatre. I saw Sarah play "La Dame aux Camélias," "Phèdre," "L'Aiglon," "La Reine Elizabeth," "La Samaritaine," "Jeanne d'Arc," and others. I saw also the first season of the Ballet Russe at the Opera, with Nijinsky and Ida Rubinstein and Karsavina, Reinhardt's production of "Sumurun," and so many other things. A wonderful place to grow up in, Paris. What things to see ! All around one is harmony of line and a richness of life and beauty. Versailles, Fontainebleau, Mal-maison, the Louvre, the Musée de Cluny, the Carnavalet, the Tuileries, the Place de la Concorde, the Comédie Française, the Luxembourg ! All things taken familiarly for granted then, but since how dearly and gratefully appreciated.

The summers were usually spent in England. Hep and I were sent to Farncombe to stay with Nanny's old sisters. These were always jubilant reunions, for Hep and I were very close and I missed her dreadfully. We had an old shed in the garden that we used as a "studio." Hep was always writing at something — poems or novels — and we both did a lot of drawing and painting. We started a magazine together called *The Arrow,* to which we were the only contributors, and the only readers were the Stennings, and Mother, who was forced each month to part with a shilling in order to procure the copy. She still has them. Only the other day, in London, Hep and I were laughing over them. We also gave scenes from plays, and concerts, our audience consisting of the dear old ladies described before, and sometimes a neighbor or two who would drop in. They took it all very seriously, and sat solemnly listening to "As You Like It" and "Ro-meo and Juliet" (in which I played Romeo to Hep's Juliet), or to our concerts, which included popular songs of which I sang the comic ones and Hep the romantic. I used to accompany her romantic renderings with the mandolin, which I had learned to play in Paris. How serious and busy we were ! And what fun we had.

I relieved these artistic efforts by joining the Godal-ming troup of Girl Guides. The Baden-Powell Girl Guides, as they are called in England, are a very im-portant factor in the lives of English girls. The organi-zation is in every way similar to the Boy Scouts, the uni-form being blue instead of khaki. I was very proud of mine, especially of my blue scout hat, on the band of which was stamped B. P. G. G. in gold letters. The members of the Godalming troup consisted mostly of children of the tradespeople around these parts, and the officers were ladies of the county gentry. We were taught all kinds of things : cooking, sewing, first-aid, botany, and of course the usual scout-lore. Every sum-mer I would compete in the contests, and displayed proudly on the left sleeve of my uniform a line of badges including interpreter, musician (representing my efforts on the mandolin !), Red Cross, horsemanship, and botany. One summer, in my effort to win the cookery badge, I put Hep and the old ladies through some trying meals which must well-nigh have ruined their digestions !

So time went on and I reached the Alfred de Musset and Byron period, was melancholy and ardent beneath a healthy and reserved exterior. How old I seemed to myself ! Youth had passed !

At this time Mother decided that I ought to have some English education, and at the end of the spring term I left the Collège Sévigné of happy memories and we set

off for England, where we were to spend part of the
summer with the Favershams at Chiddingfold, and
Mother was to look round for a boarding-school in which
I should start work in the autumn.

III

Mother and I and Bessie set off via Dieppe-Newhaven and arrived in London, where we had dinner at the station, and took a night train to the little village of Chiddingfold in Surrey. I was overcome with sleep and curled up on the seat in the train until we arrived about eleven o'clock. The Faversham's car met us at the station, and we sped through the dark country lanes toward the Old Manor House which I still thought of as home, for the Favershams always asked us to stay there a few weeks every summer, and the old house and garden had scarcely changed since I lived there as a tiny baby ten years back.

Dear Uncle Will Faversham was there to greet us with his warm vivid personality. How we loved him ! What a darling he was ; all children adored him. He was so full of vitality and fun. The two boys Bill and Philip were of course in bed at this late hour, and I felt very proud and important arriving after our long journey at midnight, and being treated like a grown-up. We went down the long Jacobean passage, with its beautiful gleaming oak beams, and turning to the left heard voices in the study ; here we found "Aunt Julie," Mrs. Faversham, known on the stage as Julie Opp, one of the most gracious people imaginable. The room was long, low-ceilinged, paneled, with French-windows opening straight out onto the great stretch of lawn. Oil lamps cast pools of warm light, and deep shadows crept out of the corners in an eerie beckoning way. There was a log fire burning brightly in the big fireplace, and seated beside it on a low stool sat Constance Collier.

I thought I had never seen anyone more lovely to look at. She was very dark, with a vivid, glowing face ; her dress was a curiously exciting color, a kind of Pompeian red, and seemed a perfect frame for her rather violent beauty. She wore no jewelry, only a big spray of magnolia blossoms pinned carelessly to her bodice. Mother had told me she was to be there, that she was one of the most successful young actresses in London and was a famous beauty, so I had already in my thoughts woven a web of glamour about her, and was rather afraid that perhaps she would prove a disappointment. But no, there she sat, in all ways perfectly fulfilling my dream of what a famous and beautiful actress should be.

We all went into the dining-room ; I was allowed to stay and have supper, as it was so late and I was hungry after the journey. As usual I sat stolidly without saying a word. I listened to the interesting talk, much of it of course about the theatre ; it was good to be there among these fascinating people, good to hear their rich, harmonious voices.

I gradually sensed that something was wrong, that they

were deeply worried about something. Mother seemed upset and shocked. I found out afterwards that our darling Aunt Julie was ill, and that the doctors advised sending her to Switzerland for several months, perhaps even a year. Mother had, of course, heard of their fears in this respect, but now she was told that there was no longer any doubt in the situation, and they wanted her to go with Aunt Julie to Arosa in Switzerland, and see her settled there. I gathered that I was to be left in Chiddingfold for the summer, with Uncle Will and the boys. I was so tired that the whole scene is confused and blurred in my memory, and directly after supper I was sent off to bed.

When I went over to Constance Collier to say good-night, she took my face in her hands and said : "I'm told you want to be an actress ?" I flushed scarlet with embarrassment at having the attention drawn to me, but managed to murmur a few words, and then was thrilled to the point of tears when she said : "You have a good voice for the Theatre. I have a feeling you'll be all right." This was the beginning of a great friendship between us. I was her slave from then on and hero-worshiped her with all the intensity of my twelve years. She said she would like to hear me read something to her and that she would work with me on some parts. I went off to bed radiant. My room was just above the study, a sweet little room all paneled in green, with an old lattice window round which yellow tea-roses clustered fragrantly.

I could hear the drone of voices talking far into the night ; they drifted up from the study below, and mingled with my dreams as I lay in my little bed, my thoughts full of the purpose of my life, my head ringing with the words of encouragement and hope, and my spirit nearly bursting with the determination not to fail what seemed to me an inspiring challenge.

The next morning, in spite of my late hours the night before, I was up with the birds. It was so wonderful to look out on the lovely garden glistening with dew, the lawn covered with magpies catching the early worms ; I thought that if I were to slip out there on the lawn, there might even be a chance of finding a hedgehog. It was certainly impossible to stay indoors, so I scrambled into my clothes and sneaked down the old passages to the back door that gave onto the shrubbery. There were so many things to investigate ; every corner of the old garden was tenderly familiar. Then there were chickens and dogs and a donkey, and I soon found to my great joy that a riding horse had been added to the menagerie.

Shouts from the nursery told me that Phil and Bill were awake, and they soon came rushing down to the garden. They were wonderful-looking boys ; Bill slim and fair, Phil dark like his father, almost like an Italian child. We were great friends, though of course being several years older I felt rather superior. They had a very sweet "Nanny," an American, to whose peace I fear my visits contributed little.

In spite of many tempting suggestions on how to spend the morning (the boys were full of plans, even a picnic with the donkey cart was suggested and I was to be allowed to drive all the way) I had my mind on more serious matters and, as Constance Collier says, "I turned up on her breakfast tray" ! Poor darling, she little knew what the result of her rash words would be, or at least she didn't dream of its being so immediate. I wanted to know what I was to read to her and what I was to study. I was certainly a determined young woman ! She got rid of me only by promising that after lunch we would read Shakespeare together : Juliet and Ariel in "The Tempest." She thought Ariel would be a good part for me to work on.

It was one of many fascinating lessons. She tried to make me see the values in the beautiful speeches, to bring out the music without losing sight of the meaning. She explained to me the two chief dangers in reading Shakespeare's verse : the one, to intone in a stilted fashion, losing all feeling of reality ; the other, precisely the opposite, in the effort to be natural, the complete disregard of poetic metre. She was a very severe critic, a ruthlessly honest teacher. I shed many tears over Ariel, on which I worked with fanatical frenzy, but even while she ridiculed me pitilessly and seldom praised, she really believed me to be talented and was convinced that some day I would do good work in the Theatre. I can never express how much I owe to her faith and patience ; not merely at this particular time in my life but consistently all through my career she has helped me with her clear and thorough knowledge of acting.　She never lies about a performance, never flatters, is careful with her praise, but when she *is* enthusiastic one can be certain that her enthusiasm is genuine, and how proud and happy it makes one feel !

The weeks flew by.　Mother had gone with Aunt Julie to Switzerland.　Life at the Manor House seemed strange without them, though there was much to do.　"Favvy" was busy working on several new productions for the New York season, among them "Romeo and Juliet" and "Julius Cæsar."　Sometimes he would rehearse scenes with Constance Collier, who was to play Portia in "Julius Cæsar."　This was always very exciting.

He wanted Mother to let me go to America and play Lucius in the production, but Mother thought I was too young to start work, that I needed further education, and refused permission, much to my dismal and bitter disappointment.　It is hard to say whether she was wise in this decision or not.　It always seems to me that the earlier you start in the Theatre the better.　Education in the conventional sense of the word is really of little value to acting ; and the years wasted can be ill spared in an art in which there is much that can be mastered only through actual practice.　I am convinced of the truth of Stanislavsky's statement in "My Life in Art" where he says it takes twenty years of work before you "begin to know anything about acting."　But of course his standard is very rightly a high one.

Many interesting people drifted down to Chidding-fold during these weeks. Henry Ainley, Forbes Robert-son, May Webster (now Dame May), Mrs. Robert Louis Stevenson, Lloyd Osborne, Anthony Hope, Maxine Elliott. They form in my mind a colorful, fascinating procession.

Suzanne Ainley was there too. She was beloved by all children. We called her "Sasha." She was full of the most delightful ideas and games and stories. I re-member the day after Aunt Julie left when everyone felt sad, she cheered us up by sending around announce-ments of an "Unchristmas Tree" party that would be held that afternoon on the tennis court. She had planted a big branch of a tree in the ground, and hanging on it were all sorts of amusing little toys and a plentiful supply of candy. Everyone received a present with a funny verse accompanying it. We all laughed a great deal and felt much better. Darling Sasha, she would go to any amount of trouble to raise other people's spirits, no mat-ter how sad she herself might be feeling beneath all her infectious gaiety.

But, alas, this magical summer came to an end, and it was now time to join Hep in London, where she was to take charge of my boarding-school outfit and see me safely deposited in Bognor, at a young ladies' educational estab-lishment that had been highly recommended to Mother and that she had finally decided upon.

Hep was then living in Wimbledon with our Uncle James Welch. He was a very great comedian ; at that time, after eight years of "When Knights were Bold," he was appearing in a farce at the Criterion Theatre called "Oh, I Say!" He was a tiny little man with a real clown's face, sensitive and squirky, and the melancholy, unhappy sort of temperament with which most great comic artists seem curiously enough to be endowed. When I think of him now, I am reminded of the famous story of Deburau. When this great clown was ill to death with nervous melancholia, the doctor who visited him, not knowing his identity, advised him as a tonic to go and see Deburau play as often as he could! What tragic irony! And so my uncle, while ill and sad, kept the British public in roars of laughter until his death several years later.

The business of procuring a boarding-school outfit was a very serious one in those days. Mother had always dressed me very simply, but with a certain charm and in colors that pleased me, usually blue. I think there must have been a conspiracy among English boarding-schools to make children look as hideous as possible, perhaps a salutary antidote to budding vanity. In any case I found myself to my amazement setting off for Bognor wearing a dark blue serge suit with a skirt nearly to my ankles, a green shirt, high-collared, the tie in the school colors of green, red and gray, a stiff sailor hat perched on top of my head bearing a band of the same charming color-combination, my hair pulled back tightly and held in a "tail" by a slide. "Sensible" shoes and pigskin gloves completed this romantic ensemble.

The train to Bognor was jammed with girls returning to their respective schools, and Hep deposited me in the charge of Miss Wall, the head teacher of Mother's particular selection. I tried hard to swallow the lump in my throat and blink back the tears that blurred my last glimpse of Hep standing on the platform waving as the train slowly drew out.

I found myself in a completely alien world. Stared at on all sides by the inquisitive and seemingly unfriendly eyes of the "old girls," we "new girls" huddled together and hid our tear-stained faces in copies of *Home Chat* or *The Sketch*, the unfailing companions of train journeys in England.

The particular school to which we finally arrived was one of many thousand of the "better schools" in England, to which little girls are packed off at the age of eight, to be released at the age of seventeen or eighteen, perfect young English ladies. To me, used to the free and responsible life my Mother had allowed me to lead, surrounded by an interesting and stimulating atmosphere, accustomed to thinking for myself, to drawing my own conclusions, to being treated, not as a child (and therefore inferior), but as a human being whose opinions were worth consideration, to me who had proudly been entrusted with a latch-key of my own at the age of eight, and had even crossed the Channel alone on two occasions, this school — smug, straitlaced and in every way conventional — seemed a dreary prison.

To my surprise, after the examinations determining

what grade one should start work in, I was placed in
the highest class with girls of sixteen and seventeen.   I
had expected to be with children younger than myself,
as my education had been entirely a Continental one.
But I soon found that the system of the Collège Sévigné
had been evolved, so that the subjects studied at Bognor
and the way they were presented, seemed to me childish
and uninspiring to a stultifying degree.

I suffered tremendously from the ugliness of my surroundings ; and the difference which the other children
sensed in me, while intriguing them, made me an "outsider," and for some weeks I was very lonely.   I was only
grateful that as a senior I was given a cubicle of my own
and there cried myself to sleep many a night surrounded
by pictures of Bernhardt, Constance Collier, and Irving
— and with my precious volume of Shakespeare under my
pillow.

I was too much of an egomaniac, however, and had too
great a sense of my own importance, to consent to being
an "outsider" very long.   I soon found that physical agility, skill in riding, jumping, running, hockey-playing, and
such things, was the measure of one's popularity.   In
this I was lucky, for I was an unusually strong and active
child, and my visits to a gymnasium twice a week during
the Paris years had developed my agility and strength to
a gratifying degree.   The girls soon discovered that I
could jump higher, run faster and endure longer than
most of them and I was gradually looked upon with increasing respect, culminating in my unanimous election

as left wing on the school hockey team, a position involving great *éclat*.

The strict and intensely dull routine of the school work, the rigid curb on behavior, the incessant vigilance over manners and deportment, were a sore trial to me. I discovered one way to "let off steam" which proved very effective.

A girl in my class (nearer my own age than most, for she was only thirteen) and I, became "chums." She had been brought up in Belgium and spoke French, which was a bond. To her I confided my discovery, which was that one could slide through a cubicle window after "lights out" down onto the fire-escape ; and from there one could climb successfully over the kitchen wall to freedom.

We would then walk rapidly to the beach and run as fast as we could on the hard moist sand, until we returned elated and exhausted and crept into our respective cubicles. The element of danger in this escapade (which we repeated often) was also invigorating, for had we been discovered we should, of course, have been expelled.

My first experience as a director really dates from my Bognor days (which, incidentally, were brief).

There was to be a school play at the end of the term. Miss Wall's choice was a play about Queen Elizabeth. I can remember it only vaguely, but I know I was cast for the part of old Lord Burleigh, an old man of around eighty ! Having been accustomed to seeing occasional rehearsals, either with Uncle Jim or at Chiddingfold, I soon discovered that Miss Wall seemed a bit at sea. The play did not progress, would not take shape, and I felt the performance would disgrace us all. Of course my theatrical aspirations were not unknown in the school, and it was also common knowledge that I came from "artistic" people and actually knew some actors and actresses ! I took my courage in both hands and applied to Miss Wall for the job of director.

I think the poor lady was really relieved, for she handed the play over to me without a murmur, and I set to work, giving as close an imitation of a director as possible.

What a performance that must have been ! I often roar with laughter at the memory. I can see myself now at the dress rehearsal, entangled in a long cotton-wool beard, for I still clung to my part of old Lord B., deadly serious and grappling madly with a lot of children who couldn't or wouldn't learn their lines, who had not the faintest idea of what a "performance" was, and who above all would not realize that it was a matter of life and death !

Since then I have been through many a mad and disastrous dress rehearsal, but I don't suppose I ever felt a more acute sense of anxiety, of grim responsibility, of dismal despair, than on this initial occasion.

THE term came to an end and I was free ! I went to London where Hep met me and put me on the train for Paris. I was to join Mother there and then we were to spend Christmas in Copenhagen.

How good it was to see Paris again !   I felt like a little wild animal escaped from a cage.

Mother had the most wonderful surprise for me : She was taking me to the Répétition Générale of Sarah Bernhardt's new play "Jeanne Doré," and afterwards we were to go backstage and I was to be introduced to Mme. Sarah.   Mother had met her through Julie Faversham, and the whole thing had been arranged.   I was so impressed that as usual on such occasions I was silent and apparently unmoved.

The great evening came.   We set off in a cab, for Mother, looking lovely, was in evening dress, and I had on my party frock.   The great theatre was packed with all the most interesting personalities in Paris.   Mother pointed out some of them to me : Cécile Sorel, Anatole France, Tristan Bernard (the author of the play), Rostand, and Ida Rubinstein, who sat in the left-hand stage box, tall and regal, wearing a huge ermine wrap with an Elizabethan collar and seven paradise plumes in her elaborate coiffure.

It was a magnificent scene !   Jewels, strange perfumes, ladies in extraordinary "creations" (the fashions in those days were anything but simple), men in evening dress with boutonnières, standing surveying the boxes and circle through their opera glasses ; animated talk everywhere.   Would Mme. Sarah be in good form ?   Would the play be interesting ?   Would it be a success ?   The clash of anticipatory opinions.   Everywhere deafening noise and confusion ; then the magical hush as the houselights dimmed, and the great crowd, like a wild beast cowed into submission, in one vast concentrated body watched the rise of the curtain.

The story of this play "Jeanne Doré" concerns an elderly woman, a widow, whose son commits robbery and murder to secure some money for the woman he loves, a married woman several years older than he, who proves heartless and mercenary. He is arrested and sentenced to the guillotine. The efforts of his mother to save him, and the agony she goes through, culminating in his death, furnished the main theme of the tragedy. The part of the boy was played by Tristan Bernard's son whose début it was in the Theatre. The mother, Jeanne Doré, was of course played by Mme. Sarah.

I shall never forget the ovation Sarah received on her first entrance. The audience rose to its feet and applauded and cheered for at least five minutes. Mme. Sarah stood there in her simple black clothes, bowed before the devoted enthusiasm of the public, until finally she was allowed to speak and the play really began.

It was a wonderful, indescribable performance : the scene where Jeanne is discovered in a crowded market, doing her shopping for the evening meal, and hears rumors of the murder, gradually piecing together from the people's talk the facts of the crime, until she realizes with terror that her son is the guilty man ; her frantic efforts to hide her agitation, as she pays for her bundles and puts them in her marketing bag, trying to appear calm and even to discuss casually the horror of the murder ;

the scene with her son in the little room at the back of the stationery-shop where she works, when he confesses and begs help ; the unforgettable scene outside his prison cell, where his mother comes to say a last good-bye through the barred grille, and where he, hearing a woman's voice, thinks at last that his mistress has come to him and calls out *"C'est toi, Fanny ?"* and the agony of the mother, crucified against the wall outside, answering *"Oui, c'est moi"* and impersonating the woman he loves, in order to give him a few moments' consolation ; then the final scene near the guillotine, where she leans against a fence, alone, knowing her son is going to his death.

This part was one of the few realistic rôles Bernhardt ever played. One was accustomed to see her in the classical furies of "Phèdre," the romantic glamour of "Marguerite Gautier," or "L'Aiglon," the tender poetry of "La Princesse Lointaine," the neurotic, passionate fanaticism of "Lorenzaccio" ; but on this evening she was suddenly revealed as a simple, modest old woman ; her performance was a miracle of realism, so touching, so unerringly well-observed, so bewildered and crushed by sheer human sorrow, that the public was moved to tears of tender compassion, and when the final curtain fell, there was a moment of poignant silence before the storm of applause broke loose.

At last the houselights went on, and there was the usual rush backstage of friends anxious to congratulate, of people curious for a glimpse of the great actress, hoping for a chance to touch her hand in thanks for the wonderful evening she had given them. My heart seemed to stop beating as Mother took me by the hand and we joined the crowd working its way slowly towards the stairs leading to a corridor connecting with Bernhardt's reception room.

I could not see the room very well : I was too small to see over the shoulders of the countless people who managed to squeeze their way into it. Mme. Sarah had not yet left the stage. With her amazing energy, in spite of the great effort of her performance, she was discussing some technical details with the stage-manager and electricians. The reception room in which we were waiting was directly connected with the stage by a short flight of steps. At last the door was thrown open and Bernhardt appeared, leaning on the arm of her beloved son Maurice. *"Bonsoir, mes amis,"* she said, *"Ah ! je suis si fatiguée je roule !"* and swaying slightly with fatigue she was assisted down into the room, where she was immediately surrounded by an excited and ecstatic mob. Mother finally managed to push her way to the fore, and dragging me by the hand she reached Mme. Sarah's side.

This moment, my first meeting with Sarah Bernhardt, was one of such intense joy that it was almost agony. I had longed for the last five years for this great event, and now I was unable to say a word, could only gaze at her with fascinated eyes. She put out her hand to me and I kissed it, as I had been told I should (for she was always treated like royalty). She smiled and bent down and kissed me on both cheeks. I remember that her teeth had specks of rouge on them from her make-up, which was very heavy, and that her eyes were laughing and a curious sea-green in color. That's all. The moment had passed, other people hemmed her in ; I felt awkward, and so ashamed. Tears came into my eyes. I had not been able to express one word of the burning admiration that seethed within me. Silently I followed Mother out into the square, into a cab. Silently we drove home and silently I crept into bed. It was not until several days later that Mother could make me open my mouth on the subject.

I must have been a singularly unsatisfactory child to her, poor darling, who by nature is gay and lively and full of bubbling enthusiasm, for whenever I was profoundly moved by either gratitude, joy, anger or sorrow, I was equally solemn, equally inarticulate.

But in my heart there was a deep appreciation, a swelling ecstasy. I had touched Mme. Sarah's hand and she had smiled at me and kissed me on both cheeks. For several days I wouldn't wash my face, till finally Mother, observing that it was dirtier than usual, applied soap and water liberally, at the same time stressing the virtues of cleanliness. I was too shy to offer the true explanation : I had not wanted to rub away the kisses of *La Grande Sarah*.

IV

IN a few days we started for Copenhagen. The journey was a long one. We went via Hamburg. For thirty-six hours we sat in our second-class carriage. Occasionally, when the train stopped long enough, we would climb down and stretch our legs walking up and down the platform, or drink a glass of cold beer at the station café. We had a food-basket, packed with delicious picnic food ; cold chicken, ham, hard-boiled eggs, cookies, and that sort of thing. It was really a great adventure, this journey, much more interesting than the less strenuous one to England.

My light fiction consisted of the complete poems of Alfred de Musset in two volumes which I had received as a pre-Christmas present from Mrs. Bodington. I was familiar with most of them, knowing many by heart, but never tired of reading them. Mother had difficulty in restraining a smile at my frivolous choice. As she would say, "Musset seemed like a dull dog to take on a forty-hour train journey" and I must confess that today I heartily agree with her !

We left the train at Gisser and crossed the Baltic by ferry to Varnemunde in Denmark. It was bitterly cold.

The Baltic was covered with a thick coat of ice, and they used an ice-breaker on the bow of the boat to open a channel through which we slowly crawled. From the ferry we boarded another train which deposited us in Copenhagen.

Mogens and Uncle Kai met us at the station and took us to the hotel. We went directly over to see "Bet." The darling old lady sat waiting for us, with her best shawl over her frail shoulders, her best cap on her white hair (she always wore little black velvet caps embroidered with jet beads), and the inevitable piece of needlework in her tiny worn hands.

Copenhagen at Christmas is a joyous place. Nowhere else have I seen the spirit of holiday so freely and charmingly expressed. All the streets are decked out with garlands of pine, holly and mistletoe. The gay Danish flag, scarlet and white, flies from windows and flagpoles ; the bright lights of the festive shops fall on the crisp snow and make it shine with a thousand diamonds. With pots of scarlet tulips, large anemones or crimson poinsettias (called in Danish "Christmas stars") in most of the windows, and with a Christmas tree in every home, the whole quaint town exudes an atmosphere of jolly, warm hospitality.

The Christmas dinner was to be at Uncle Kai's on Christmas Eve at six o'clock, immediately followed by the tree and presents ; in Denmark it is the custom to celebrate on *Jule Aften* (Christmas Eve) rather than on the twenty-fifth itself. Mother and I called for little "Bet" and took her with us. It was a real Danish family dinner : Uncle Kai and his wife Anna, Mogens and his little sister Gerda, Bet, Mother and I. Danish people as a rule are gay, lively, warm, and emotional, and the little party was animated and noisy with expressions of happiness, affection, and goodwill.

The dinner was an important business. First there was the excitement of who should find the almond in the *risengröd* (a sort of rice porridge with which the meal began). The lucky one received an extra present, and I'm sure that my little grandmother always saw to it that the coveted almond turned up in my plate. The prize was, as I well knew, a large pear of marzipan, a candy which I particularly doted on. After the *risengröd* came many other marvelous dishes, until the roast goose was carried on amidst loud applause, decked with tiny Danish flags and stuffed with prunes and apples. Then there were delicious Danish cakes, candies, and fruit in plenty.

The merry repast came to an end, and in old Danish fashion each one went up to the head of the house and said *"Tak for mad"* (Thanks for the meal), to which Uncle Kai smilingly answered *"Velbekomme!"* (May good come of it !) He then opened the big double-doors leading into the drawing-room, where the tree stood glistening with tinsel, stars, flags, and candles.

Then came the presents. Cries of delight — of surprise, laughter and tears, for a Danish Christmas is never complete without tears. This time it was an old silver dish (which for many years had been in Grandmother's family and which she presented to Mother) that started them off. Mogens and I had felt sure this *would* start the tears, and it did. Mother received it from Bet with a glowing face and taking her little old mother in her arms burst into sobs of appreciation and tenderness, the others all cried a little, then laughed at each other for being so silly, then cried a little more, until the merriment was finally completely restored by the discovery that old Ingeborg, the maid, was standing with her apron over her face crying too, all because it was Christmas Eve.

Darling, sweet, genuine people! How full of life they were, how glowing with kindness and humanity.

The days flew by. Mogens and I skated every day in Frederickborg Have, a lovely park not far from the centre of the town. We would walk along swinging our skates, taking deep breaths of the cold crisp air ; the sun would be shining brightly on the green copper roofs of the churches, Thorwaldsen's museum, and the old castle. I loved the little houses along the canal, painted in bright colors, pink, green, blue, or yellow ; the sea-gulls would whirl in great clouds over the water, and when the ice was too thick for them to procure food, they would tap at the window-panes with their beaks, begging for help.

In the evenings we would sometimes go to the Royal Theatre to see a play or an opera. Or we would spend the evening with Bet, listening to one of her stories ; perhaps of how, as a young girl, she had crossed over to

Sweden in a sledge at a time when the ice was very thick on the sound. Or, perhaps, to tales of the invasion of Schleswig-Holstein by the Germans ; or old sagas of the Vikings. She had a fascinating repertoire of which we never tired.

My birthday came on January 11th, and I was to attend my first ball, given in my honor by Uncle Kai. I had a new dress for the occasion, new shoes, and long gloves, and was given some flowers to wear. I felt completely grown up.

There were a great many children invited, school comrades of Mogens' and their sisters or friends. The boys all wore evening dress, with short knickers and silk stockings and patent leather pumps. Mogens had on a white piqué waistcoat, against which glowed impressively the gold watch chain his father had given him that Christmas. I thought he looked very handsome. A tall boy, very fair, with great serious bright-blue Nordic eyes.

We opened the ball together, for the whole affair was very seriously and correctly handled. We had little cards on which to write down our dances, blue for the girls, and pink for the boys.

Being the guest of honor, and being a foreigner who had lived in Paris and London, who spoke several languages, who was to be an actress and who had even met Sarah Bernhardt (Mogens had given me good publicity !), I soon had my card filled up, and I was never off my feet. Although I felt shy and self-conscious at first in my new clothes and my new rôle as the centre of attention, I soon

thawed out and had a wonderful time. We danced on
after supper till four in the morning, and I was taken
home by Mother happy and exhausted and feeling that
thirteen was a wonderful age to be, and that Copenhagen was the most delightful place in the world.

AFTER this exciting and glamorous holiday Bognor
seemed a dull place indeed ! We played hockey, pur-
sued our useless studies, and took long walks in crocodile formation, two by two, through icy lanes.

But I was not to stay there long. Mother took pity
on me and to my great joy removed me back to Paris
before the end of the term.

Miss Wall was heard to remark after my departure that
now perhaps she might have some peace, for "she had
not known whether she was on her head or her heels"
during my brief sojourn under her austere roof ! Poor
Miss Wall ! Looking back over the years I find in my
heart a sort of pitying affection for her ; children are
cruel and thoughtless ; hers was no easy task.

An added delight was in store for me in the news that
Hep was to spend a year with us in Paris. It was good
to have her again. We took up our old tasks. *The
Arrow* flourished again, and Mother was regaled with
many entertainments in the evenings. I went to the
theatre a great deal and worked very hard in my room,
acting, always acting. I thought of nothing else.

Whenever I felt discouraged and momentarily lost
faith, I would walk to the Boulevard Péreire and stand

in front of Bernhardt's house in the hope that perhaps I might catch a glimpse of her. Somehow the thought of her dauntless, untiring personality stimulated me into a more robust mood, and I would walk home again, with the renewed determination to work hard and follow my dreams.

One marvelous day Mother informed me she had received a letter from Julie Faversham who wanted me to take a personal message to Mme. Sarah. Darling Aunt Julie realized what a great joy this would mean to me and thus gave me the opportunity of meeting Sarah again. A telegram arrived from Mme. Bernhardt's secretary saying that she would receive Mrs. Faversham's friend in her dressing-room after the matinée of "Phèdre."

Clutching this precious document, I went to the theatre and bought a ticket in the *poulailler* (the equivalent of our peanut gallery) and ascended the many stairs on winged feet.

Anyone who has had the good fortune to see Sarah Bernhardt's performance in "Phèdre" knows how amazing it was. Anyone who has not can *never* know, for it is useless to try to describe it. It was probably the greatest of all her rôles.

As the play drew to a close, I was trembling with terror at the thought of having to go backstage, but at least this time I would really have to speak to Mme. Sarah, for I took very seriously my rôle of messenger.

It was quite a journey from my high seat in the *poulailler* to the magical door that led to her apartment. When

I arrived the door was open and there were several people in the reception room, though of course few compared with the crush of an opening night.

A cross-looking gentleman with a jet black moustache and a red face tried to prevent me from entering the room. I brandished the telegram in his face. He read it and, giving me a look of amused surprise, told me to come in and wait till he should fetch me. Mme. Sarah would see me in her dressing-room. I sat quietly behind a large palm-tree that stood in front of the window, and from there observed the room.

It was of good size, paneled, with little furniture, obviously a mere anteroom used mostly as a buffer to protect the rooms beyond, the last of which was the dressing-room proper. Other secretaries were working away getting rid of people with polite excuses; several people came from the inner rooms where they had been privileged to talk with Mme. Sarah, and the anteroom gradually cleared.

Suddenly I heard a man's voice say, "And where is Mme. Le Gallienne? Mme. Sarah is waiting to see her now." My friend with the black moustache discovered me behind the plant and laughingly escorted me through the second room, a charming library, into a brilliantly lighted room, where before many mirrors stood a huge dressing-table littered with innumerable articles of make-up, and seated before it, still wearing her "Phèdre" costume sumptuously weighted with jewelry, a jeweled diadem on her head, her face covered with a heavy make-up, was Mme. Sarah. Standing in a row along the wall facing the mirrors were several men and women : her maid, a couple of secretaries, her coiffeur, her doctor — in short, the whole Bernhardt retinue.

The gentleman with the moustache solemnly announced, "Mlle. Le Gallienne, the friend of Mme. Faversham !"

Sarah looked at me in amazement and burst into merry laughter. *"Mais, Mon Dieu, c'est un bébé !"* she cried and put her arms round me, hugged me and kissed me on both cheeks.

It took me some moments to recover from the mortification of the general laughter, which though kindly and good-natured made me shrink into myself. But Mme. Sarah soon put me at my ease. She sensed my discomfiture and in an effort to make me comfortable asked me many questions, gradually drawing me out, until to my surprise I found myself chatting with her quite easily. She kept my hand in hers and I looked with wonder at her finely modeled, nervous fingers, covered with rings, the tips painted scarlet to the middle knuckle. I delivered my message and received the answer, with many protestations of affection for dear Aunt Julie.

Sarah was amazed to hear that I was by myself, and at first would not consent to my returning home alone. I assured her that I was accustomed to taking care of myself ; I was so afraid she would appoint the black-moustached gentleman to accompany me, and I longed to walk home in peace, so that I might live over again each moment of this magical interview. It was difficult to convince her, for like many people in the Theatre, themselves used to a life of unconventionality and freedom, she was extremely strict in her ideas about bringing up children, and I believe her own grandchildren found her more straitlaced in regard to them than many a grandmother of the Faubourg St. Germain would have been. She finally gave in, with many warnings to me to be careful crossing the streets and not to talk to strangers, and, kissing me again and filling my arms with flowers, she handed me over to a secretary who escorted me to the stage door below.

Here I found the usual crowd waiting for Mme. Sarah's departure, and pushing my way through with some difficulty I started home feeling as though I were walking out of a dream.

RAPIDLY the years went by. I remember I spent a summer in Denmark and Sweden. There I stayed with my cousins the de Neergaards who had a big old farm near Gottenborg. My youngest little cousin, Beatrice de Neergaard, is now a talented member of the Civic Repertory Theatre. During all this time I can recollect nothing eventful. The next vivid incident that stands out in my memory took place in 1914 when I was fifteen years old.

Constance Collier had kept in touch with me during these years, every now and then sending me a brief and exciting word from America where she had been touring with Faversham. These notes were always full of encouragement and messages of her continued faith in my future. Suddenly a letter came from London, saying she was to produce Maeterlinck's "Monna Vanna" for some special matinées, and should we be planning to be in London that summer, she would like me to "walk-on" in the production as her page, and thus I could make my first appearance in the theatre with her. This was wonderful news and as Mother had fortunately arranged to be in London at that time, I was able to write back a glowing letter of acceptance.

Mother and I had been invited to spend some weeks at the house of an old friend of ours, Ralph H. Philipson. He was a very wealthy Englishman who had married an American. For years they had been among Mother's closest friends, and we were both devoted to dear R. H. P., as Mother always called him.

For the past year he had been through the awful tragedy of his young wife's illness, which all his care and all his money could not seem to cure. She had died early in the year and he was bitterly unhappy. His friends flocked to him, full of loving pity. He was such a beloved man, so simple, sensitive, and kind.

He lived in a huge apartment on Portland Place, and in spite of the many guests, he seemed lonely and forlorn. He had always been a great lover of the Theatre and was tremendously interested at the news of my approaching début.

Rehearsals were to start immediately. I was called to

the Queen's Theatre and was put through my paces in
the mob-scene at the end of the third act. I also had an
entrance in the first act, where another page and I were
to carry Constance Collier's train. There were a great
many professional "supers" involved in the production,
and as a rule we were rehearsed separately by the stage-
manager, until the rest of the play was ready to be synchronized with the mob-scene during the last days of work.

The day before the dress rehearsal Mr. Philipson said
he had some shopping to do, and would I accompany
him ? Of course I was delighted, though I didn't suspect
his real purpose. We drove to Clarkson's, at that time
the most famous wig-maker and make-up vendor in London. Still unsuspecting, I followed R. H. P. into the
fascinating shop ; on all sides were wigs, masks, theatrical
costumes ; the walls were covered with hundreds of
photographs of actors, and the atmosphere was heavy
with the smell of pomades and grease paints.

R. H. P. went straight up to the counter where make-
up boxes of all sizes and shapes and splendors were on
show. Selecting the largest and most splendid box of
all, he turned to me and remarked casually, "I thought
you'd probably need a few odds and ends to make up
with tomorrow ; and you *must* have something to keep
them in, don't you know." He then called Clarkson
over and told him to fill the box with everything I could
conceivably need in the Theatre. Clarkson did a good
job. I think, by the time he got through, that box
contained enough make-up to last me many years, cover-

ing the widest range, from a "fair young girl" to a "robust old man" !

I was speechless with delight. This was so typical of the way R. H. P. did things. He was the most generous man in the world and adored making presents, but he was so shy that he was always terrified of being thanked for anything. We got on famously, for he understood my inarticulate gratitude just as I understood his inarticulate giving, and we were mutually relieved.

Before leaving the shop, knowing my adoration for Bernhardt, he pointed out a picture of her, hanging in the place of honor, on which Sarah had humorously inscribed *"Mon cher Clarkson, vous êtes le Bonaparte des perruquiers, vous êtes le* Napoléon *des costumiers !"*

On the drive home he told me of seeing Sarah play in her youth ; at this time he was a man of close on sixty. I confided to him my great dream of possessing a copy of Mme. Bernhardt's "Memoires," but they were out of print and extremely difficult to procure. I had noticed a copy of this book in his library and asked if he would lend it to me over a period of time, so that I might copy it by hand. He looked at me smilingly and said, "Won't it be rather a job ? It's quite a long book, you know." (It was indeed about eight hundred pages long.) But that evening he handed it over to me and laughingly wished me luck. I shall never forget his amazement when eight months later I returned it, at the same time showing him a great pile of manuscript in my own still childish hand. I had copied every word of it, and on the last page had placed a happy and exhausted "Finis."

He took my copy and had it bound for me in two splendid volumes of blue and gold, and it still reposes on my bookshelf, now bearing an inscription which Bernhardt wrote in it some years later : *"Chère et adorable enfant, je suis émue de la grande peine que vous avez prise à copier ce grand travail. Je vous souhaite un grand bonheur dans votre vie et je vous embrasse tendrement !"* It stares at me from the shelves, a monument to what has sometimes been called my "incorrigible stick-to-itiveness !"

But to return to "Monna Vanna." The opening performance arrived, with its usual excitement. The dress rehearsal had gone badly and everyone was comforting everyone else with the old stage saying : "Bad dress rehearsal means a good first night." This, I have discovered, is not infallible, but in this case it proved true.

I dressed in a big supers' room with about fifteen or twenty others. I had no idea of how to make up, but the other actors, with the unfailing kindness shown to "beginners," gave me hints, and I dare say I looked no worse and no better than most young creatures who for the first time get their hands on a box of make-up, let alone *such* a boxful as Clarkson had provided me with. My wig looked rather odd, I thought, and it was difficult to get my rouge on without making it blotchy — it would *not* seem to blend, though I worked for hours with my new hare's-foot which Clarkson had not forgotten to include.

I feel like crying when I think of that hare's-foot. I used it in the Theatre steadily for sixteen years ; by that time it was a sad-looking object, but I knew every hair on it and was so accustomed to the "feel" of it in my hand. Then it disappeared. I suppose some "cleaning-lady" thought it a dirty old thing and threw it out. How I miss it !

I was spoiled dreadfully on this my first appearance on any stage. Messages came to me from Uncle Jim, Henry Ainley, the Favershams and Sasha. Dear R. H. P. and Mother sent me flowers. I began to feel like the most important person. Five minutes before "Overture" was called, I rushed down to Constance Collier's room, and with the most perfect disregard of her nerves, and of the fact that after all it was she and not I that was to carry the brunt of the performance, I invaded her dressing-room and taking possession of her mirror proceeded to put a few last touches to my wig, which would *not* seem right to me. Instead of throwing me out, she helped me with the utmost patience, and watched me in smiling amazement. Utter thoughtlessness, utter selfishness of extreme youth !

The performance was a great success. Prinzewalle was played by Lionel Atwill, then a young beginner whom Constance had discovered. They were both recalled time and again at the end of the play. The next day the notices were fine, and it was decided to extend the few afternoon performances originally announced to an evening run. This was good news to me, who could not bear the thought of leaving the world of the Theatre, and it was arranged that I was to stay over a few weeks longer in care of Mr. Philipson, while Mother went back to Paris, where Mme. Fédora's business awaited her.

It was Mother's intention to send me to Munich, where I was to study music and other things. She still felt I was too young to start playing and insisted on my having further education. She little dreamed that a great monster was shortly to be let loose on the world, and that personal plans, however well made, however excellent, would be wiped away in the chaos and horror of the Great World War.

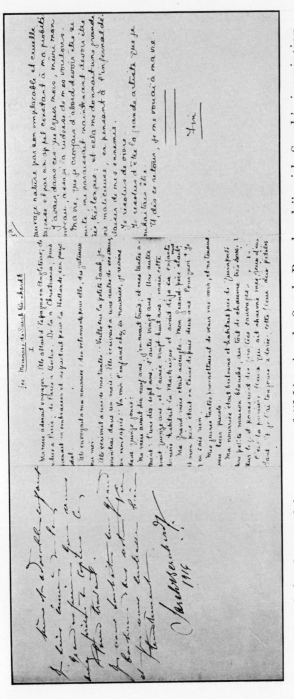

Facsimile of the first and last pages of "Mémoirs de Sarah Bernhardt" with Sarah's inscription

At 15 with Hep

V

THROUGHOUT these busy days, full of rehearsals, of life in the Theatre where I felt so completely happy, rumors reached me, *war*-rumors ; there was trouble, *grave* trouble ; but of course everyone ended, "It won't come to anything. No such thing as a *war* could be in this day and age ; we are far too civilized." But "civilized" though we imagined ourselves to be, the War came. Then "It'll be over in three weeks," everyone confidently remarked. No one was really worried ; people were surprised and rather excited ; it was a new sensation. No one took it very seriously at first. Poor England ! Little did she realize then what it was to cost her !

The run of "Monna Vanna" was to end on the Saturday, and I was just leaving the theatre after the matinée when Mother appeared. I had thought her in Paris. She was very grave. The thing *was* serious, then ! She told of the hysteria in Paris, the exodus of foreigners. The banks were besieged, the stations jammed with people trying to get away. Her one thought had been to join me. She had closed up everything in the rue Tronchet, and with one small handbag had waited for hours at the station to get a train to Dieppe where, for hours longer, with hundreds of others, in the pouring rain, she waited on the pier for the boat which brought her to England. She was ill with exhaustion and worry. There was nothing to do but wait and watch developments ; surely the thing *could* not last more than a few months !

Mr. Philipson invited us to stay at Portland Place for as long as we liked. He was only too happy to have us, he said ; it would be a splendid thing for him, as he was so lonely. The darling ! He well knew that Mother had perilously little money set aside, and that the hat business would not be a flourishing concern during this time. But he wanted us to feel we were doing him a favor by staying. What we should have done without him for the next year I cannot imagine, though I'm sure that Mother with her usual gallantry would have managed somehow. As far as I was concerned, I decided that it was high time for me to start work, and on the Monday morning after "Monna Vanna" closed, I looked for a job.

I had become friendly with one or two of the other members of the company, especially one, who had been very good to me. She had guarded me carefully against things she felt I was too young to hear or see and had helped me in many thoughtful ways. This was Agnes McCarthy, who is now a member of the Civic Repertory Theatre. I shall never cease to think with gratitude of her kindness to me in those far-off days. We had heard that supers were needed at His Majesty's Theatre for some big spectacle, and presented ourselves early in the morning at the stage door. There were already about a hundred others waiting anxiously. No luck ! We went over to Covent Garden to see if people were needed there. No luck ! Mother finally heard of these attempts and was emphatic in her desire to have me wait a while before going seriously into the professional Theatre. Mr. Philipson suggested that I should be sent to Tree's Academy for training, and this plan Mother enthusiastically endorsed. I doubt if, without Mr. Philipson's aid, we should have been able to afford it, but it was arranged and the day set for the entrance examination.

Tree's Academy was in Gower Street. In those days it in no way resembled the impressive institution it has since become under the name of the Royal Academy of Dramatic Art. The director is still the same — Kenneth Barnes, a brother of the great English actresses, Irene and Violet Vanbrugh. Three old houses had been thrown together forming a rambling building in which there was one small auditorium with a raised platform as a stage — very little equipment, in no sense a "theatre." Then there were many small and large rehearsal rooms, a dancing hall where the fencing was also taught, dressing-rooms, and, in the basement, a long, low dining-room, with a counter on which sandwiches and buns were displayed and behind which presided an enormously fat woman we called "Henny," who dispensed indigestible dainties at reasonable prices.

There must have been a great many students there,
for the place always seemed to me like a busy bee-hive.
We were divided into juniors and seniors — in other
words, first year and second year. The seniors were
looked up to as gods and looked down on us in turn with
suitable contempt. There were many classes : dancing,
fencing, voice production, elocution, delsarte (this included pantomime and stage-falls) ; and then of course
we worked on plays, which were performed in the auditorium now and then for the benefit of relatives and
friends.

There was also a class in French plays ; this was op-
tional, but of course I chose to belong, and since my
French was exceptionally good, I had the opportunity to
play all the best parts in the performances. Selfish pig !

Some of the accents in these French performances
were beyond description. I made quite a hit in a little
one-act play by de Banville called "Le Baiser" in which
I played Pierrot. I had copied my Pierrot make-up
from a picture of Sarah in "Pierrot Assassin" that I found
in a book at Mr. Philipson's. He and Mother came to
see the performance. R. H. P. had seen Sarah play "Le
Baiser" at the Comédie when she was at the height of her
fame. He teasingly told me that, while I did "awfully,
awfully well," he found her performance somewhat superior.

At Tree's Academy I first had my try at Juliet. I was
cast for the "clock struck nine" scene, with the nurse,
and the farewell scene was put up to the trial-rehearsal,

the one winning the "trial" to play at the performance. I worked very hard on the preparation for this contest, in which I believe there were four or five competitors. The rehearsal was to take place in one of the smaller rehearsal rooms.

It was a very cold morning. London was blanketed in fog ; a smoky coal fire smoldered dismally in the grate, and the room smelled of soot — an inspiring atmosphere for the passionate warmth of Verona and for those magical lines :

> *Wilt thou be gone ?   It is not yet near day :*
> *It was the nightingale, and not the lark,*
> *That pierced the fearful hollow of thine ear ;*
> *Nightly she sings on yon pomegranate-tree :*
> *Believe me, love, it was the nightingale.*

It meant so much to me to win the chance of playing this scene. I was quivering with nerves and a desperate resolve to be the winner. I was the last to play.

That morning something happened to me for a few brief moments. I started the scene and remembered nothing until I "woke up" with the tears pouring down my face, and, shaking with emotion, fled into a corner and sat down. There was a silence in the small room. I felt I must certainly have been dreadfully bad. Then I heard the teacher's voice quietly say : "I think all of us will agree that Miss Le Gallienne should play the scene at the performance. It was beautiful, my dear," and she came over to me, and to my amazement there were tears in her eyes ; and when I summoned courage to look round at the others, I saw they had been crying too.

Poor Miss Barnett, she worked hard with me from that day on, fully expecting that at the performance I would duplicate my rehearsal which they had all liked so much. Alas ! At the performance I was stiff and unmoved, I could not get away from myself. The rehearsal had been a fluke, but I had no technique of emotion, and it was beyond my power to recapture the agony of grief that had somehow poured through me at that first attempt.

We had a short holiday at Christmas and then went back to work. I had become a sort of assistant property-man, dresser, and errand-boy for the seniors, and in this way had insinuated myself into their dress rehearsals and was backstage during their performances. They tolerated me because I made myself useful. There were several students in the senior group that year who have since done fine work : Miles Malleson, both as actor and as playwright, Constance O'Neill, and Norah Balfour, the last an actress of unusual talent.

I was cast for a cockney part in one of our plays there. I forget the play, but the part was small, though of good quality. I was very familiar with the cockney speech, for during the last months, I had been working in the evenings as a Girl Guide, in one of the auxiliary war kitchens that supplied the overtaxed hospitals with broth, gruel, and other invalid foods for the wounded. They were pouring into London now : "The Old Contempti-bles," remnants of Kitchener's first "little army."

One evening I had met with a Girl Guide walking along Portland Place in uniform. I had been longing to help a little, in the War, but being so young there was nothing I was allowed to do. She told me of the soup-kitchen and I went with her to the Captain of her patrol, in charge of the particular kitchen where she worked. They were all cockneys there : the girls, the officers, everyone. It was wonderful training for me. Every evening I would leave the Academy at six, run home and have dinner on a tray in my room, put on my uniform and set off for the kitchen work in Charlotte Street. We sometimes worked there till midnight. Fortunately for the poor Tommies, we didn't *actually* do the cooking, only kitchen-maid work. But I learned a lot about cockney there, and it stood me in good stead in my new part at the Academy. In the audience, the day of the performance, there happened to be a producer, Lyall Swete. He sent for me a few days later and offered me a cockney part in a play called "The Laughter of Fools" that he was producing for Frank Curzon.

I SHALL never forget the sensation of standing on the stage of the Prince of Wales Theatre being looked over for the part of the cockney slavey, Elizabeth, in "The Laughter of Fools." Lyall Swete was a kind and charming man. He made it as easy as he could for me, but I kept hearing a voice from the dark pit of the auditorium calling out : "How is her height compared with Squires ?" and "Can she whistle a tune ?" and "Better run her through the scene in the last act ; if she can do that, she can certainly play the rest of the part." I learned that this mysterious and terrifying voice was that of the manager, Frank Curzon. Then to my horror I was asked to take my shoes off. I well knew that I had a hole in my stocking at the big toe. Still, I must succeed in securing the job. I decided to swallow my pride and took off my shoes with an air of the greatest composure. I was grateful that no one laughed, or seemed to pay any attention to the hole. The stage manager thrust a part into my hand, and I read the scene, not knowing what it was all about, but using a cockney dialect as I had been instructed. I had a feeling that the part was a good one and prayed that the awe-inspiring gentleman out front would be satisfied with me. Then I was told to whistle "Snooky Ookums," a popular song of that period. Whistling had never been one of my star accomplishments, and, because I was so nervous at that moment, my lips were hard and dry, and it was most difficult to produce a sound. I bravely made the attempt, and produced a rather breathy and faltering version of "Snooky Ookums" which was greeted with hearty laughter by the invisible and all-important gentleman in the stalls. I thought, of course, that this was the end of all my chances, and that I would be told to go away and never, never return. Lyall Swete told me that would be all, and I scrambled into my shoes and made for the stage door trying to swallow back my tears, for I was certain I had failed dismally.

Mr. Swete called me just as I was slipping out : "Where

are you off to ? I haven't told you about the rehearsal call !"

I could scarcely believe my ears. Was it possible they were going to accept me ? He came over to me and put his hands on my shoulders : Mr. Curzon had been delighted with my reading, and I was to report for rehearsal the following Monday. I was to receive three pounds a week for salary and was to call at the office for my contract.

It was too wonderful to be true. I felt bewildered and passionately grateful. My one thought was to rush home and tell the great news to Mother. She was very happy, and R. H. P. was delighted too. It was a Great Day ! We decided that I was to send in my resignation to Tree's Academy and leave at the end of the week, for rehearsals would, of course, take up all my time.

On Monday the work started at the Prince of Wales Theatre. It was a fairly large company, including some excellent players. Old Alfred Bishop had the leading part, that of a dear old man henpecked by his wife, an overbearing kind of woman played with great humor by Frances Ivor. Of course at the end of the play he comes out on top, much to the satisfaction of the public. The leading man was Ronald Squires, and the cast included Violet Graham, Hilda Trevelyan, Jack Hobbes, and several others. They were all wonderfully kind to me, and did everything in their power to help me, realizing that I was just a kid and a very green beginner. I especially loved old Mr. Bishop, a darling man and a splendid actor.

We rehearsed for about five weeks, from ten in the morning till six in the evening. Lyall Swete was a very pleasant and courteous director to work with. He handled me remarkably well, for he realized that with my utter lack of experience it was wiser not to brusque me nor frighten me with too many technical instructions. He had cast me to type and trusted that if left largely to my own instinct, I would give him the values he felt to be right for the play. All my faults suited the part perfectly ; my awkwardness, my clumsy movements, my rather deep, monotonous voice, my solemnity, all of these were just what he needed for the character of the little cockney slavey. It was a very grateful part for me at that time ; for though comic, it had to be played in deadly earnest, and the more seriously I played it the funnier the effect would be from the front.

The dress rehearsal was over. Constance Collier was there, and as usual gave me encouragement and some useful hints. Everyone seemed pleased with me, and I felt happy, for I had worked with the greatest conscientiousness.

The day of the opening I did not feel in the least nervous ; I only hoped that I should be able to do exactly what Mr. Curzon and Mr. Swete wanted. I had no thought of making a personal hit ; it never occurred to me. I hoped that old Mr. Bishop would, and that the play would be successful enough to deserve a long run. I had my eye on that three pounds a week !

Mother took me to dinner at Lyon's Restaurant opposite the theatre, and from our table near the window I
could see the big electric sign announcing "The Laughter
of Fools" by H. Maltby ; but this somehow seemed to
have no connection with me and I was able to tuck away
a large meal, much to Mother's amazement. She, I fear,
fared less well ; she was nervous enough for the two of us !

I was excited to think that darling Nanny would be
at the performance. She was working somewhere outside of London, and I seldom had a chance to see her.
I went over to the theatre very early, and in my dressing-
room, which I proudly occupied by myself (in those days
they did not forget the comfort of their actors), I found
messages of good luck and some flowers from Mother and
dear Nanny.

The call-boy called the overture and the play started.
My first act consisted of nothing but "yes'm" and "no'm,"
in answer to various questions put to me by my mistress,
Miss Ivor. To my surprise, I no sooner made my entrance and said the first "yes'm," than I heard a strange
sound from the house ; it was like a roar, grew and
mounted in volume, then faded away again. Instinctively
I waited each time for this exciting roar to subside before
continuing the scene. It was some time before I realized
what it was : it was the laughter of the public, and I was
told on my first exit that I was getting over my points
beautifully.

It had never occurred to me that I should be laughed

at, for to me there was nothing funny about Elizabeth ; I thought of her as rather a tragic part.   But seeing that Mr. Swete and all the company seemed pleased and delighted with the result, I felt reassured.   All through the play, on each entrance, I was greeted by this same friendly laughter, and again every time I opened my mouth ; and when my last exit came, I heard the sound of applause and wondered what had happened, for I knew the end of the play was still several minutes off.   I was told that the applause was meant for me.   I had received my first exit hand.

At the final curtain the audience was enthusiastic.   I had been told to take two curtain calls with the company, and then to my surprise, old Mr. Bishop took me by the hand and led me onto the stage, where he left me to make my first solo bow.   I remember looking out into the dark house, and seeing something white fluttering in the first balcony.   It was darling Nanny, who, bursting with pride, found clapping insufficient and was waving her handkerchief madly.   This was the only time Nanny ever saw me play (she died a year or two later), but always at opening nights, I look for that waving handkerchief and somehow feel that in spirit she is there.

The next morning Mother came in with her arms full of newspapers.   She was radiant : it seemed I had made a real hit.   One review pleased her especially, it was headed "Brilliant New Comedienne" and next to the heading was my picture.   It was all very breath-taking.   The result of my success was quickly felt.   I was interviewed

William Faversham

"Pierrot" in "Le Baiser"

by several papers, was asked to take part in all-star bene-
fits of which many were given at that time for the War
charities, and received at least seven offers from other
producers to appear under their management as soon as
my contract with Curzon terminated.

Business was bad in the theatres and growing worse ;
the Zeppelin raids, to which London was to grow so accustomed, had just started and were not conducive to
theatre-going. In order to mislead the enemy the parks
were left brilliantly lighted, and the crowded thorough-
fares were in medieval darkness ; it was almost impossible
to find one's way at night. The War was going badly
for the Allies, and in spite of their dauntless magnificent
spirit the Londoners were depressed and sadly worried.
The wounded kept pouring in, the fresh troops were
shipped by tens of thousands to the front, and the casu-
alty lists grew to ghastly proportions.

Since I had become a professional actress, I had been
forced to give up my night work in the kitchen with the
Girl Guides, and like all the other people of the Theatre
tried to help do my bit by taking part in countless entertainments for the wounded, for the Belgian Refugees, of
whom there were many thousands in a huge camp at
Earl's Court, and for the young recruits in the training
centres. One of the most indefatigable workers was Constance Collier. She organized a huge benefit performance
of "Peter Ibbetson" at His Majesty's Theatre for the Red
Cross. The best-known stars of the London stage took
part in it ; Henry Ainley and Owen Nares played the

parts played in this country by Lionel and Jack Barry-more, and Miss Collier played the Duchess of Towers, in which she is so gracious and moving. She asked me to take the little part of Victorine, the French girl, and so for the second time I had the joy of working with her.

After about six weeks, "The Laughter of Fools" came to an end and I found myself faced with the momentous decision of a next step.

I had three choices : to go on tour with the play as Elizabeth ; to accept one of the several offers I had received and stay on in London ; or to make a very drastic move which somehow fascinated me by its novelty and promise of wider horizons — to leave Europe and try my luck in America.

I had always been intrigued by the thought of America. I had heard so much about it in the old days from the Koopmans, and more recently from Constance Collier and the Favershams. I thought of it as a vast free country of inexhaustible possibilities, where the opportunities for work would be greater and more varied. We had heard from the Favershams that "The Laughter of Fools" had been bought by David Belasco, who expected to produce it in New York in the autumn, and that in view of my London notices, I would have a good chance of playing Elizabeth under his direction.

Mother left me to make my own decision. I think she might have preferred me to remain in London, where I had made a hopeful start, and where my prospects seemed secure. But security has no special charm for

extreme youth ; I felt the desire for adventure and decided to start off for the Great Unknown Country where
I felt sure fame and fortune awaited me.

At that time, on account of submarines, the only boats
one could safely cross on were American, and we took
passage on the S. S. *St. Louis*.

I shall never forget the excitement of our preparations. We had been in London a whole year, a long
time for us to be in one place, and this was to be a
real journey ; the little *St. Louis* took two weeks to make
the crossing. In one way I felt miserable at the thought
of leaving Europe, the familiar ways and places, the many
dear friends. I think Mr. Philipson felt quite sad too,
as we sat down to our last dinner at Portland Place. He
had casually left a beautiful dressing-case in my room.
"Thought it might come in handy, you know." It was
a beauty ! I had always dreamed of possessing just such
a case. It was of green crocodile skin with gilt fittings,
and on each fitting was engraved *E. Le G.* in Mr. Philipson's beautiful handwriting. What a joy it was to arrange all my belongings in the various bottles and jars
and boxes ! At last it was packed to my satisfaction, and
proudly turning the key, I grasped it firmly (for I would
let no one else touch it !) and went down to the car.
Mr. Philipson saw us safely settled in the train, and having supplied us with magazines, candies, and eau-de-
cologne for the journey to Liverpool, wished us God-
speed.

VI

THE *St. Louis* can scarcely be described as a magnificent
boat ; for anyone used to the great transatlantic liners it
must have seemed very small and uncomfortable, but I
had never been on anything larger than a Channel
steamer and so was sufficiently impressed. We had a tiny
inside cabin on E deck, the lowest on the ship, well beneath the water-line. There were two bunks in the
cabin ; I took the top one, Mother the one below me.
It was difficult to arrange our possessions comfortably
in the tiny space provided, but we finally dug in for the
voyage, which was to prove an immensely exciting one
for me.

I learned to my great jubilation that Elsie Janis and
her mother were to be on board. Elsie was one of my
very great admirations. I had seen her play the year before in that never-to-be-forgotten "Passing Show of 1914"
at the Palace Theatre, and again this year in the "Passing
Show of 1915." All London went mad over this fascinating and bewilderingly talented young American
star. Her versatility, her charm, her marvelous dancing
— now eccentric, now graceful — her amazing imitations
took the town by storm. My first meeting with Elsie

Janis occurred after a matinée at the Palace Theatre, when I, with the usual hundreds of others, waited outside the stage door to catch a glimpse of the star as she left the theatre. Her car was waiting and I managed to wiggle through the crowd till I stood directly beside it. As Elsie stepped into it, accompanied by her mother, I heard her speak in perfect French to her maid, and seizing this opportunity I said to her : *"Vous parlez français merveilleusement, Mlle. Janis."* She looked at me with those bright piercing eyes of hers and laughed. Then she asked me my name, which was familiar to her as she had read my father's poems. Mrs. Janis, with her unfailing kindness to young people, suggested that I come and visit Elsie in her dressing-room after a performance. This I did, of course, in a very few days, and having surmounted my first access of shyness, told her about myself and my aspirations. This was the beginning of a friendship that I am proud to say continues to this day. The thought of the Janis's kindness to me through the years fills me with immense gratitude. Imagine my joy at the discovery that on this, my first trip to America, we were to be fellow-passengers.

The first few days were very rough, but being an excellent sailor, I was on deck most of the time. Elsie and I had many talks in all the different languages and dialects we could muster. We used to walk round and round the promenade deck, and each time round we would talk in a different language or in English with a different accent, much to the bewilderment of many passengers, who felt dizzy enough as it was, for the boat was bucking like a bronco. What fun we had ! About half-way across it became stiflingly hot, and Mother and I found our cabin rather trying. Several nights we slept on deck. The days passed pleasantly enough, and in the evenings there were dances, or card-games, and finally the usual ship's concert, at which Elsie sang and danced and gave imitations. I've often wondered what the concert would have consisted of if it hadn't been for her !

At last the great day came when I was to have my first glimpse of New York. We were to dock about noon. I couldn't sleep all night with excitement and anticipation. I was up and about at six o'clock already packed, and the hours that followed seemed interminable. It was a scorching day in mid-August. I had never felt such heat, but was too happy and interested to care. There was a heavy haze over the city, and we were well into the har-bor before the magical profile of New York crept out of the mist. I had often been shown pictures of it, and had had it described to me, but could never have imagined such a curious, fantastic sight. It was unlike anything I had ever seen, so utterly individual and strange. I gazed on in silence ; I could not analyze my impressions ; I felt awed and a little frightened.

Then came the confusion of landing ; the noise, which seemed to me louder and more strident than any noise I had yet heard ; the unfamiliar twang of the voices, the tense, slightly strained faces ; and over all, the sense of hurried purpose. Everyone seemed to be striving to go somewhere or achieve something with the utmost possible speed. My impression crystallized gradually into the words : noise, speed, immensity, machinery ; the whole imbued with a curiously exciting vitality.

William Faversham's business manager met us and steered us through the customs. He was a pleasant man, and must have been efficient, for within half an hour we left the pier and found ourselves outside in the broiling sunshine. He had explained to us that on account of the heat wave Favvy had thought it advisable to rescue us from the city, and we were to join the Faversham family at Mattituck on Long Island, where they had taken a house for the summer. He had sent the car for us and we were to drive straight out there at once. We drove up Fifth Avenue and over the Fifty-ninth Street Bridge. I was too confused and awed to speak, but Mother and Favvy's manager talked of the great changes that had taken place in New York since her first visit to America with Father the year before I was born. She was amazed at the new buildings, at the rapid and extraordinary development of the city. The length and size of the Fifty-ninth Street Bridge filled me with wonder. How strong one would have to be to fight a place like this, I thought to myself. I felt crushed, insignificant, and suddenly homesick.

It was a long drive. The beauty and difference of the countryside soon helped me into a more stalwart frame of mind, and by the time we arrived at Mattituck I had quite recovered my good spirits.

It was good to see Uncle Will, Aunt Julie, and the boys. The house was very large, with a good-sized park, and there was also a long stretch of private beach. It was a splendid place to spend a holiday. Uncle Will insisted that we should stay out in the country during the hot weeks following. He said New York was dead and that all theatrical activity was out of the question for the moment.

Many interesting people came to Mattituck. I remember meeting Edward Sheldon there, and Channing Pollock; also the poet, Ella Wheeler Wilcox. Dear Favvy tried whenever he could to push me to the fore; he was determined that I should "make good" in America.

Much to our disappointment, we heard that Belasco had given up the idea of producing "The Laughter of Fools," for the time being at least, and I therefore would have to search for some other job. This was really a great blow, for we had practically no money and I was completely unknown in New York.

The Favershams moved into town in early September. They had a lovely old house on East Seventeenth Street, and Mother and I stayed with them a few days while looking for a place to live. The hotels were so expensive; but on the other hand we had no furniture of any kind, so could not take an apartment. Then Favvy hit on a wonderful plan. We were to take a small flat in a house next door to his on Seventeenth Street and furnish it with theatrical furniture from his storehouse!

The house in question was an old walk-up apartment house, where we secured three small rooms on the top floor, with kitchen and bath, for twenty-six dollars a month. Here Mother and I settled ourselves, surrounded by a quaint and motley assortment of furniture : chairs from "The Barber of New Orleans" were coupled with a table from "Herod," curtains and a chest from "The Fawn," and a few odds and ends from "Othello." It was the most amusing place, and somehow Mother managed to keep everything from clashing and achieved a harmony in this little home that would have seemed impossible to anyone less endowed with her particular talent for home-making. We couldn't afford a maid, but Mother, with her usual courage, undertook the cooking and washing, while I looked after the rougher work of scrubbing and scouring. Then in the afternoons I would make the round of the offices in search of the elusive job.

Favvy was wonderful ! He took me round himself and introduced me to many managers and agents. They were kind to me for his sake, but seemed consistently unimpressed, and the general feeling was that I was too English in type for the American stage. My London notices left them all cold ; New York was far away from London, and what the British liked was a matter of small importance to them. It was a gloomy outlook ; we couldn't afford to return to England, and our little store of money was ebbing fast. To make matters worse, my dear Uncle Will had to leave for a tour, and I felt desolate.

In order to cheer me up, he sent for me to join him in Toronto, Canada, where, as a tribute to the British, he recited some patriotic poems at the end of his play, which was "The Hawk" translated from the French success "L'Épervier." He wanted me to recite the Belgian poem "Carillon" in French and some other English things. This week in Canada, and the feeling that somebody still believed in my stage possibilities, were a great comfort to me. It was good of Favvy to have thought of it, to have realized the help it would be to my sinking spirits.

On my return to New York I was at last summoned to the office of a manager. I went with a beating heart to this interview. Harrison Grey Fiske was producing a play from the Hungarian, "Mrs. Boltay's Daughters," with Rita Jolivet as star. There was a small bit and some understudies. On account of the number of parts allotted to me to cover, I was offered the surprisingly high salary of fifty dollars a week. Rehearsals were to start immediately. I rushed home to Mother jubilant; I had no inkling of what the play was about; neither did I know what bit I was cast for. I only knew that they had thought I would do, and that I had actually "landed" the engagement.

I went to the first rehearsal with a light heart. There one of the greatest surprises of my life awaited me : the bit I was cast for was a colored maid ! It was a terrible predicament ! I had scarcely even *seen* a colored person, let alone heard one talk. My speech was hopelessly — and seemed at that time irrevocably — British. What could I do? I had to hang on to that job at all costs. I was in terror of being fired the first time I opened my mouth. In despair I looked around the hall in which the rehearsal was to take place. I knew no one in the large company. Over in a corner I saw a tall, dark, young woman who seemed to have a kind and gentle face. She caught my eye and gave me a friendly smile. In a second I was at her side explaining my plight. She laughed heartily and said she would help me. Fortunately the bit consisted of very few lines, and while waiting for the rehearsal to begin, she taught me the words, which I repeated as best I could parrot-fashion. The result must have been amazing! I shall never forget the terror of hearing my cue and of having to say my first line before the assembled company! The young woman who helped me so kindly was Merle Maddern, a talented actress, and ever since that day one of my greatest friends.

How I ever kept the part I don't know ; it has always been a mystery to me, but keep it I did, and on the opening night I presented the astonishing portrait of a colored maid with very bright blue eyes shining out of a smeary chocolate-colored face, and speaking a grotesquely bewildering dialect : part British, part cockney, with here and there a dash of Irish.

"Mrs. Boltay's Daughters" had, alas, but a very short run — alas, that is to say, for the fifty dollars a week ; for those not having enjoyed the delights of blacking-up for a part cannot realize how dubious such delights can be ! It is impossible to keep really clean ; all one's clothes bear the inevitable signs, and one is forced to live in a skin several shades darker than one is accustomed to.

Once more the search for the elusive job began. Each day I "made the rounds" and each day brought the usual disappointments. My great solace was to slip into the Public Library between visits to various offices ; I was in the midst of a veritable orgy of reading. I had discovered Whitman, and, even more important, I had at last discovered Ibsen.

A couple of years before this Mother had given me "Brand" to read, but in translation, which inevitably betrays much of its force and richness. At this time I came across a volume including "The Master Builder," "Hedda Gabler," and "A Doll's House." I was obsessed by these plays, particularly by "The Master Builder," and went on to read all the others.

I had formulated a list of parts which I made up my mind I would play before the age of thirty-five. This ambitious list consisted of : Hilda in "The Master Builder" and Hedda in "Hedda Gabler" of Ibsen ; Peter in Barrie's "Peter Pan," Marguerite Gautier in "La Dame aux Camélias" of Dumas, Juliet in "Romeo and Juliet," and the Duke of Reichstadt in Rostand's "L'Aiglon." Quite a modest goal ! In the meantime, while working in my mind on all these plays, I needed a job, and one I was bound I would find.

I had heard that Austin Strong, whom I had met one evening with the Favershams, had written a play in which there was a cockney part of the type of the slavey Elizabeth. I felt that given the opportunity to read for the author, I might have a chance of securing the part, for I was at least sure of my cockney. But my friend Favvy was on tour, and there was no one to take me to see Austin Strong. There was no time to lose, for the play was announced to go into immediate rehearsal under the management of William Harris, Jr. I made up my mind I would call on Mr. Strong, and the same day set off.

I called at his home and explained my purpose to the maid who opened the door for me. A few minutes later I was received very kindly by Austin Strong, and begged him with great earnestness to give me a reading. He consented, at the same time explaining that he had not the final decision on the casting, but should he like me in the part, he promised to procure a hearing for me with Mr. Harris, the manager, and Mr. Lewis Stone, the star. He then left me to myself to look over the manuscript for a few moments.

At first glance I knew that come what may, I *must* win the part : the play was called "Bunny" and was set in England in the early nineteenth century. The cockney servant, Jenny, seemed to me an even better part than Elizabeth ; it was more obviously a comedy character, though in his writing Mr. Strong had succeeded admirably in bringing out the curious tragi-comic quality so typical of many cockney types. Burning with the intensity of my purpose I read several scenes and succeeded in gaining Mr. Strong's enthusiastic approval. He told me to go to rehearsal the following day at eleven o'clock and assured me I should then have an opportunity of reading before Mr. Harris. Mother and I spent the evening in great excitement, feeling hopeful and trying hard not to anticipate elation.

The try-out took place in Daly's Theatre on Broadway, now torn down. The old house, fallen from its days of glory, was in disuse except for occasional rehearsals ; it was dusty and shabby, yet the stage and auditorium held a dignity and charm that no amount of neglect could successfully hide. I sat down behind an old piece of scenery to wait my turn and take my bearings. Several other characters were being tried out before Jenny. Mr. Harris, Mr. Strong, and Lewis Stone were seated in the orchestra, and one by one the different actors were rehearsed in various parts, the stage manager holding the book. It was several hours before he announced that the readings of Jenny would begin. There were three or four applicants. I can remember distinctly being amazed at their attempts at cockney ; this accent is as difficult for an American as, I had learned to my cost, a negro accent is to an English person. There was one actress who seemed very experienced, who instantly gave the outline of an amusing and colorful performance and I was devoutly glad that her cockney was the worst of the lot ; had it been otherwise I felt sure I could not have stood a chance.

My turn came, and feeling very small and pitiably lacking in outward assurance, I walked onto the stage. After my first scene a voice out front said : "Her cockney accent isn't very good, is it ? — The last one seemed to be better." Was it possible I had heard correctly ? If there was one thing I felt certain of, it was that my cockney was genuine ; they could say I was too young for the part, too clumsy, too ugly, too monotonous, anything, *anything* rather than that the other lady's cockney was better than mine ! I smarted with anger under such an injustice, and as usual when angry, felt the tears rising in my throat. Mr. Strong persuaded the others to hear me through to the end, and also to let me rehearse again on the following day. I was his choice for the part.

The next day I felt oppressed and uneasy ; the rehearsal was an agonizing experience. At last it was over and my worst fears were realized when Mr. Strong came to me on the stage and taking me to one side explained, with a kindness that still could not soften the blow, that Mr. Harris did not find me suitable for the part. I was too inexperienced and my cockney did not convince him. I did not dare speak, I was terrified of betraying my utter misery ; smiling grateful thanks, I looked up at my friend through the tears that would come crowding out no matter how hard I forced them back, and without a word shook him by the hand and went rapidly out into the street. I did not dare let myself go till I was safely home, where I indulged in a really good cry.

Mother was as indignant as I at the aspersions cast on my cockney ! We consoled ourselves by re-reading my London notices, in which there was not one criticism of my dialect, and decided the reason it was not thought convincing here was that in America they were only used to hearing bad cockney and could not recognize the genuine article when they heard it. Having come to this conclusion, in which there may have been a grain of truth, we felt infinitely better and turned our eyes once more toward future opportunities.

In search of further consolation I called up the Janises, who were then at Philipse Manor, and told Elsie the whole dismal tale. They very sympathetically invited me to come right out and spend a few days in the country, and Mother, knowing it would cheer me, packed me off.

This was one of many wonderful visits I made to the historic old house, Philipse Manor, where Elsie and her mother for years dispensed a warmth of hospitality difficult to equal. I was one of the many hundreds who turned to them in search of help, of renewed courage, of invigorating wisdom and kindness, and like the many hundred others, I was never disappointed. In a day or two I had completely recovered my spirits and felt prepared once more to grapple with New York. I was to return to town next day. After lunch I was called to the telephone. Mother in great excitement told me that Mr. Austin Strong had been searching for me, that after having tried over twenty others in the part, they had finally concluded I might be the best after all, and that I was to attend rehearsal the next morning !

Rehearsals started in earnest. We worked as a rule in a gloomy building called Bryant Hall, on Sixth Avenue near Forty-second Street. There are many large rehearsal rooms there, rented by the hour to managers when stages are scarce. There are usually two or three big musical-comedy choruses at work there, besides jazz-bands and orchestras ; the noise is deafening, and the building seems dirty and depressing. However, I was to play Jenny and nothing else mattered.

I used to take the subway at Eighteenth Street, get off at Times Square, and walk to Sixth Avenue. Rehearsals began at ten-thirty and continued till one ; then, after a half-hour for lunch, were resumed until five. I was very often kept on till six to be drilled in my part by Mr. Harris and Mr. Stone. I had my lunch at the Auto-mat next door where for ten cents I could procure a large cup of coffee and a gigantic cinnamon-bun, which I found was the most filling thing to be had for a nickel.

I always dreaded being kept on after the rest of the company was dismissed. Mr. Harris made me terribly nervous, and the more nervous I became the worse I would be in the part. Instead of realizing this, he kept at me relentlessly, making me repeat a scene over and over again till I felt like crying. Now that I look back on it all, I can see that far from meaning to be unkind, he was only trying to help me ; he was fearful of my lack of experience and worried lest I should let the play down by lack of attack. Lewis Stone used to stay on at these sessions, for most of my scenes were with him, and I shall never cease to be grateful to him for his considerate understanding and patience.

One evening as we were leaving the building, he caught up with me on the stairs and said : "Don't you get rattled now ! Just follow your instinct and you can't go wrong !" He had seen my flushed face as I slipped out of the hall and wanted to give me a word of encouragement. I was passionately thankful to him ; he seemed to have faith in me, and I so needed that faith at a moment when I felt everyone else distrusted my ability. From that moment on, my devotion to him was unwavering, though of course inarticulate ; and today when I sometimes see him play on the screen I always say in my thoughts : "Thank you, dear Lewis Stone ; from my heart, thank you !"

We were to open out of town and play two weeks before coming into the Hudson Theatre, New York. This was the first time I traveled with a company alone. My salary, which was again fifty dollars a week, made it advisable to leave Mother behind in our little home. We opened on Christmas Eve in Elmira, New York. It was a hectic business : we arrived there in the morning, had a dress rehearsal all day lasting till past seven, and, without taking off costumes or make-up, swallowed sandwiches and coffee in the dressing rooms. The curtain rose at eight-thirty on the first performance.

It was a packed holiday house and the public were in a jolly mood. The play went over very well ; we were all jubilant. It was a splendid company including such well-known actors as Henry Stephenson, Hilda Spong, Gypsie O'Brien, and Claude Beerbohm. I had a hand on two of my exits, and everyone was very kind to me ;

Mr. Harris, much relieved, came back and told me I had
done well ; I felt that this was praise indeed and wrote
Mother a happy account of the evening.   The notices
next day were good, and praised Lewis Stone and his company highly.

We went on to Rochester, then to Syracuse.   The performances went well.   In the daytime we rehearsed, making slight changes here and there, tightening up the
tempo, adding finishing touches for the all-important
New York opening.

The company were cheerful and friendly.   On New
Year's Eve we played Syracuse and after the performance
had a festive supper at the Onondaga Hotel.   It was all
very jolly and I had an exciting and happy time.   Everyone was so pleasant to me and spoiled me delightfully.
We all felt hopeful of the play's New York success and
were in high spirits.

At last the great evening arrived.   I had spent a large
part of the day in the Hudson Theatre, arranging my
dressing room and unpacking my make-up and clothes.
That evening, after the performance, the Favershams
were giving a supper for Mother and me.   Favvy had
returned to New York for the holidays, and he and Aunt
Julie were coming to the performance with Mother, and
bringing Marie Tempest with them ; afterwards we were
to return to the old house in Seventeenth Street for the
supper party.   Mother had worked hard to make me a
new dress which I was very pleased with.

On my arrival at the theatre that evening, I found

among other messages a wire from the Janises saying :
"Dear Eva go in and win we know you can and will love
Elsie and Mother." I determined to have a good try. I
was more excited than nervous and was anxious to get
going. The play was received with great enthusiasm,
and everyone thought it was surely a success. After the
final curtain the stage was crowded with friends of the
author, producer, and actors ; congratulations filled the
air : it was a gay and happy evening.

The supper at Favvy's was a wonderful event. I sat
at the head of the table and everyone made a fuss over
me. How they all spoiled me, bless them ! Marie
Tempest praised my performance, and laughed on hearing I had not felt very nervous. "Just you wait," she
said, "till you *know* a little more about it ; the nervous-
ness will come, and instead of getting better as the years
go on it will grow worse and worse !" How right she
was ! How absurd and touching I must have seemed to
her in my joyous ignorance.

In the morning I rushed out eagerly to buy the papers.
So much depended on the notices being good ; but of
course they would be ; everyone had thought the play
charming and the performance excellent.

Mother and I read one notice after another in growing dismay, not daring to look at one another. Alas !
We had all been fooled for the first (and unfortunately
not the last) time by a first night house of friends. The
critics, remote and unmoved, told a different story ; the
notices were, everyone of them, bad !

Mr. Harris tried bravely to keep the play alive, but it was of no use. And much to everyone's disappointment it closed in two weeks. I remember it as being full of quaint charm, and that Lewis Stone gave a beautiful performance, but I suppose it was not robust enough to survive.

Once more the search began, and this time landed me in the office of George C. Tyler. He asked me if I could talk with a brogue, and of course I answered "Yes," though I wasn't sure whether I could or not. I had seen Laurette Taylor play "Peg o' My Heart" in London at least a dozen times, and thought I could manage a fairly good imitation of her. In any case I intended to try, so I went to rehearsal as directed, again at Bryant Hall, and read the part.

The play was "The Melody of Youth" by Brandon Tynan. The author was playing the leading part himself, and the leading lady was Lily Cahill. The play was thoroughly Irish, the air was thick with "acushlas" and "alannas" and "divil-a-bits." I tried to talk like everybody else, and this, combined with my memories of "Peg," seemed to work out, for I was given the job. It was a different sort of part this time ; an Irish ingenue, the first ingenue I had ever tackled. It was interesting to try something new. I was delighted and worked very hard. My salary had now mounted (owing to my vast experience !) to seventy-five dollars a week. If only the play would run, Mother and I thought, we should feel like millionaires !

It was a very pleasant company to work in. George Tyler is a darling ; everyone loves him who has ever played for him. The day of the dress rehearsal he kept calling to me from the back of the theatre to "speak up !" and afterwards he told me he was pleased with my performance, but to be sure and speak loudly. He also felt my voice was a bit heavy for the part of a girl of sixteen and insisted on my using my upper register, which in those days I had no control over whatsoever. The result must have been most unpleasing to the ear, I should think, and I used to come off after every performance with an aching throat, for I had no idea how to produce my voice in any key but the one I ordinarily used. However, if it pleased him I was willing to try anything.

There was one other terror in the play for me : I had to burst into a merry peal of laughter in the middle of the second act ! There is nothing in the world harder for most beginners to do than to laugh, and I was not the exception proving the rule. From the beginning of the act on I would be preparing myself. I thought of nothing but that dreaded laugh. By the time the cue for it came, I was so tense, so tied up in agonized knots, that no noise would come at all, or if a noise did come, it resembled the braying of a donkey more than the laughter of an ingenue !

How they kidded me about it ! And then each member of the cast would try to help me ; all had different advice which I tried out in turn, and occasionally all at once, with appalling results. I kept the cast in convul-

sions over my efforts. Of course the solution of merely
seeing something funny and laughing at it never occurred
to me ; I was not sufficiently relaxed for that. It was
during my work in this play that I began the never-
ending pursuit of relaxation ; and what years and years
of work it takes to catch up with this invaluable element
in acting ! A few happy beings are born with it, but the
majority of beginners and young players have to battle
with tenseness every inch of the way for years. Beginning with a general tenseness from top to toe you work
until it is eliminated in everything but your hands ; you
succeed in chasing it out of them, and find it turns up in
your toes ! If you banish it from your throat it will
lodge in your solar-plexus, effectively killing all true flow
of emotion ! And then of course there is the dreadful
feeling that you alone are afflicted with this curse, and that
all the fine actors you see around you, so at their ease,
with such graceful, flowing movements, were endowed
with these enviable assets from their first step on the
stage. I remember several years later reading Stanislavsky's book "My Life in Art" (an invaluable book for
young actors, it seems to me), and finding out to my joy
and encouragement that for twenty years this great actor
fought for the relaxation which he at last so perfectly
achieved.

"The Melody of Youth" had a creditable success and
ran at the Criterion Theatre for a good four months. It
was a great relief to Mother and me ; the strain of intense

poverty was lifted for the time.   We were able to start
a savings account, and felt quite prosperous.

It was through my playing in "The Melody of Youth,"
bad as it must have been, that I was chosen for my first
leading part.   Harvey O'Higgins and Harriet Ford, authors of "The Dummy," "Polygamy," and other successful plays, had written a new one called "Mr. Lazarus"
which Helen Tyler (no relation to George) had accepted
for production.   They were searching for a young actress
to play the lead, and came in to the Criterion to look me
over.   I received a letter from Miss Tyler's office asking
me to call, and there I met the authors and Miss Tyler
assembled to observe me at closer range.   To my surprise, the moment I opened my mouth to greet them
they exchanged amused glances, and finally Mr. O'Higgins explained the mystery by saying : "Thank God, it
isn't your real voice you use in 'The Melody.'   That
was the only thing we were dubious about."

It was a delightful play, "Mr. Lazarus," and the part
of Patricia Molloy was splendid.   I felt so proud to think
they were willing to entrust it to me.   It was a particularly grateful rôle for me at that time, for it was more of a
character part than a straight ingenue ; the Cinderella
quality in it, the mixture of comedy and pathos, the wist-
ful awkwardness of the girl, were all fairly well within my
restricted range.   It was a lucky day for me when Miss
Tyler sent for me.

I started rehearsals while still playing in "The Melody

of Youth," which was due to close in a couple of weeks. To my delight I found that Florine Arnold who had given an inimitably comical performance as an old Irish aunt in the "Melody," had been chosen for the part of my mother in "Mr. Lazarus." She had always been very good to me and was pleased that I was to play such a fine part as "Pat."

Florine Arnold was one of the funniest actresses I have ever seen. She had been in many successes, among them "Mrs. Wiggs of the Cabbage Patch" and "Mrs. Bumpstead-Leigh," in which she appeared in support of Mrs. Fiske. Her appearance alone would cause the house to roar with laughter, and she was a wonder at comical make-ups. She was a small, fat, round little person, with the tiniest hands and feet imaginable, a chubby round face with round eyes and a tiny round nose. She was good-natured and sociable and I spent many hours listening to amusing stories of her experiences in the Theatre, of the many interesting and well-known stars she had worked with.

Miss Tyler found difficulty in casting the star part in the play, that of Mr. Lazarus. At last they secured Henry E. Dixey ("Adonis" Dixey). A young man almost as inexperienced as I, played opposite me ; his name was Tom Powers. We had some delightful comedy scenes together. I liked him immensely ; he was so gay and good-natured and played with such unaffected sincerity that it was a joy to work with him.

Rarely have I known such pleasant rehearsals. The

authors and the manager were gentle and courteous and did all in their power to make one feel happy and at ease. In this way they managed to get the best out of their little company, for we all adored them and could not work hard enough to bring their play to the hoped-for success. We opened at the Belasco Theatre in Washington, D. C. It must have been late May or early June, for I remember walking with Tom Powers after the performance in the lovely little park opposite the theatre. The magnolia trees were in bloom and I was introduced to fireflies, which I had never seen before. Tom and I were very happy ; we had both of us made big hits, we had had splendid personal notices, and the play seemed so successfull that Miss Tyler had decided to send it to Chicago for a summer run, before bringing it to New York at the opening of the new season.

The Chicago opening confirmed the Washington success ; marvelous notices for play and cast, Tom and I again praised to the skies.

All through one of the hottest summers on record, we played to crowded houses. Mother and I were jubilant ; we found life very delightful. I was made much of ; we met many charming people who entertained us royally and prophesied a great future for me ; I began to feel I really knew something about acting, took myself very seriously, and altogether must have been insufferably spoiled.

We were to play a week in Atlantic City before the New York opening which was set for August, at the

Shubert Theatre.   Although there was a feeling that it was too early an opening and also that the theatre was too large for that intimate type of play, the Chicago success had raised the confidence of the management and they felt they could well afford the risk.   Harvey O'Higgins, Miss Ford, and Miss Tyler came to Atlantic City to look over the performance, which they had not seen for several months, and gave us a good talking to, Tom and me especially ; in their opinion we were both overplaying and had lost much of the sincerity which they rightly felt was the main charm of our performances.   Young and lacking any knowledge of technique, we had not known how to seize and hold the spontaneity of our original portrayals.   A few chastening rehearsals having been administered, we returned to some degree of humility, much to the improvement of our playing when the New York first night took place.

Here we were due for more spoiling by the critics, who enthusiastically placed us in the first rank of young American actors.   I was a second Maude Adams, Tom was a second John Drew.   The truth was that we were two foolish, hopelessly conceited children in dire need of having our ears soundly boxed.   Fortunately for me, my box on the ears was not far off, and a good sound box on the ears it proved to be !

In spite of splendid notices and its fine Chicago record, "Mr. Lazarus" was a failure in New York.   Miss Tyler did all she could to keep it going, but finally had to give in after a five weeks' run.   We were all of us heartbroken, not only on our own account but for the sake of our beloved manager and authors. It had been such a very happy time for the whole company. I couldn't bear to think of working under another management, but it had to be done. I had several offers, and chose what I thought seemed the best. It was a play by Owen Davis called "Mile-a-Minute Kendall," to be produced by Oliver Morosco and directed by Robert Milton. I was to be the leading lady and was offered a good salary and a six weeks' guarantee.

It was not one of Mr. Davis's best plays, though it had a good deal of popular appeal. My part was a fairly stereotyped ingenue lead, but possessed a few redeeming features that saved it from hopeless saccharinity. The leading man was a young actor called Donald Gallaher, who showed great promise.

I immediately liked working with Robert Milton. His direction was intelligent and sensitive and his manner quiet and helpful. He was much interested in directing young Gallaher and me and seemed very hopeful as to the final result of our work. He believed in us both and showed his faith by allowing us to handle situations in our own way ; he never showed us what to do, merely suggested moods and ways of projecting them, and stimulated our own imaginations into action. I had great admiration for Gallaher's talent and enjoyed playing with him immensely. Mr. Morosco never came to the theatre ; he was to see the play for the first time at the dress rehearsal in Stamford. We were to open there, and go on to Hartford and New Haven to try the play out before bringing it to Broadway.

The dress rehearsal started and, all unsuspecting, Gallaher and I started to play quietly and sincerely as we had under the guidance of Mr. Milton during the rehearsal weeks.

At the end of the first act we were called onto the stage. Mr. Morosco was disgusted : we had no "pep," we had no "punch," we were enough to send the audience to sleep ; what did we think we were playing — "Romeo and Juliet" ? Something must be done and that quickly too, or the play was doomed before it opened. Mr. Morosco himself would take the rehearsal.

I think I have seldom been more miserable than during the hours that followed. Every point that we had worked so hard to perfect, every nuance, every note of tender sincerity, every pause, the whole musical fabric that Mr. Milton had woven with such care, all was discarded and shattered. In its place were substituted speed, noise, pep, punch and the other ingredients that, particularly at that time (sixteen years ago), were considered essential to the success of a Broadway production.

Mr. Morosco was certainly quite right from his angle ; we had just been speaking a different language. It was impossible for Gallaher and me to achieve the desired results, try as we would. We had neither of us sufficient experience to change the whole mood and temper of our performances at will. We were hopelessly and irretrievably confused. On the opening night we played abominably and rightly received bad notices. The rest of the try-out was torture to me, for I realized that my performance was a thing of wood, wholly lacking in spontaneity or truth of any kind. I was dismally unhappy and well prepared for the final blow : "the box on the ears," when Mr. Milton informed me sadly that I was "fired."

Coming at this time, at the very beginning of my New York career, being fired was a serious set-back. The managers instantly lost faith in me, feeling, with every right, that my success in "Mr. Lazarus" had been a fluke ; for of course they all heard reports of my impossible performance in "Mile-a-Minute Kendall."

These were sad days for Mother and me. But what a salutary blow it was to me, after all ! Every bit of conceit was knocked clean out of me and as I sat licking my wounds and preparing for renewed combat, I realized what a silly fool I had been, realized the full measure of my ignorance, and saw the immensity of all I would have to learn if I was ever to be allowed one day, many years from then, to serve the Theatre with some degree of competence.

People were very kind to me and tried to console me. I can't refrain from quoting Harvey O'Higgins's beautiful letter, which gave me great comfort. He writes :

"Dear old Pat :

"I've just heard — with what disgust you can imagine — that Morosco has no more sense about you than I supposed he would have. It's the same darn problem that we all have to struggle with in any art in this country — or I suppose any other.   The artist desires to depict reality, and when by some happy miracle he is allowed to succeed, all these people are delighted, and say, 'Now come and do it for *me*' ; and as soon as you begin to do it for them, they cry, 'No, no!   Not that way !   Do it *this* way !   Put more pep into it.   Give it a punch !   Wow-wow !'   I have been through it so often with publishers and editors — as well as with the purveyors of your profession — that I am, as you know, quite bald, as wrinkled as Voltaire and as bad-tempered as the devil.   For Heaven's sake, dear girl, don't let yourself become even as I.   You're much too young for it.

"Give my regards to your *mère*.   And cheer up.   We are all proud of you and confident of your future and sure that no amount of managerial Blockheadism can keep you back. With all sorts of affection and high hopes —

"Yours sincerely,
"Harvey O'Higgins"

But in spite of these and other encouraging words, the fact remained that I was without work and could not succeed in finding any.   Finally through the thoughtfulness of Harriet Ford and Mr. O'Higgins I was given my next job.

The Coast rights to "Mr. Lazarus" had been procured by B. C. Whitney, who planned a tour of the play through California and Arizona, with William H. Crane as star. My old part of Pat was offered me, and as Mother and I both felt that a change from New York would be welcome, and as I loved the part of Pat dearly, we decided to accept and started for the Coast in February.

Just before leaving New York I was sent for by a new management, under the direction of Alexander Leftvitch. He had a play called "The Daisy" translated from the Hungarian by an Englishman. The setting of the play had been transferred to London and the characters were mostly cockney. They did not think of producing the play until late spring, possibly early fall, but wanted me for the leading girl's part and were anxious to settle their plans well ahead. I was fascinated by the play. The part of Julie cast a spell over me, and I longed to have the chance of playing her. It was a type of play far superior to anything I had hitherto worked on ; one might almost call it a great play. Everything was arranged, and I took the manuscript with me to the Coast, happy in the thought of appearing in such a production.

In the meantime there was the excitement of the journey to occupy one's thoughts, the eagerness to see more of America, the anticipation of playing in strange places. I found there were two changes in the company : Suzanne Morgan replaced Florine Arnold, and Raymond van Sickle took the part Tom Powers had played. They were both very nice people and the journey out to the Coast was a very pleasant one. Mr. Crane was to meet us in San Francisco. I shall never forget crossing the Rockies in freezing weather, with masses of snow on all sides, and then gradually descending the slope into California, where little by little the warm, heavily scented air rose to greet us and we found ourselves surrounded by orange and lemon groves and flowers in reckless profusion. And then the wonderful ferry-crossing into San Francisco, just at sunset. As I leaned against the rail and looked across the bay at the approaching city, I prayed in my heart that this place would be as kind as it was beautiful, that I might work well and in some measure regain my self-respect as a player.

The next day we were called to rehearsal at the Columbia Theatre. Mr. Crane proved to be a kindly old gentleman, small and very agile for his age ; I believe he was then over seventy. We became great friends at once and I enjoyed working with him. He played the part with more gentleness than Dixey had, but with perhaps less humor. His scenes with me were more poignantly affectionate and his comedy softer and more human. He was not so sprightly as Dixey, but more lovable.

After a couple of rehearsals, when we were better acquainted, he took me to one side and confided to me that he occasionally "had trouble with his lines," and thought it would be a splendid idea if I learned all of his part as well as my own, for then I would be able to prompt him whenever he needed it. It was no extra work for me, since I knew every word of the play by heart, and I readily consented to his plan.

It was no extra work, but it was certainly splendid training ! There was scarcely a performance when the

darling old man did not forget some lines, and always in
different scenes !   I was kept busy keeping my mind and
emotions on my own mood, and at the same time holding myself in readiness to "slip him the line" when I saw
that S. O. S. look in his eye !

San Francisco liked the play ; we were there two weeks,
and then came some weeks of one-night stands, bringing
us to Los Angeles where we were booked for one week.
After this came several weeks of "one-nighters" that took
us into Arizona.   Mother found this sort of travel a little
strenuous and decided to stay in Pasadena in a little
furnished bungalow we rented there.   I was to join her
at the end of the tour for a couple of weeks rest before
our journey back East.   I remember with delight that
trip through Arizona.   There was a wild arid beauty
about the country, quite unfamiliar to me, which I found
immensely exciting.   I liked it much better than California, which seemed tame in comparison.   It was terribly hot, a fierce dry heat.   On the short jumps Mr.
Crane would sometimes invite the company to drive with
him in an open touring-car from one town to the next.
Everywhere we met with the most extraordinary hospitality ; in fact this quality in the American people, particularly in the West, struck me forcibly.   They did not
look askance at strangers, as people are so apt to do in
England ; they were vastly interested in them, and opened
their homes and their hearts with an almost child-like
warmth and abandon.

Bisbee, Arizona, stands out in my memory with especial

clarity.   There is a great copper-mine there, the "Copper Queen," I think it is called.   We had played Yuma the night before and arrived in Bisbee very early in the morning.   I had only one thought — to go through the mine.   Leaving my suitcase at the station, before even looking for lodgings, I went to see the foreman and asked to be allowed to visit the mine.   All the men were very nice to me ; I borrowed a pair of overalls and started on this exciting tour of investigation.   Down the ladders we went, down into the earth for what seemed like miles. Then through the low corridors glittering with wonderful colored metal stars.   I even persuaded them to let me crawl on all-fours into one of the new galleries, at the end of which was a miner picking away at fresh veins of ore.   Every workman we passed I would greet with the news of our performance that night, and an injunction to be sure and attend the play !   I think a lot of them did, for I was greeted with warm applause on my entrance and the reception that night was particularly hearty.

The theatre was in a dilapidated condition, and the stage so small and badly equipped that we had to cut down some of our scenery in order to fit it in.   The dressing-rooms were infested with enormous rats who seemed to have a passion for grease-paint ; two of my sticks of paint disappeared, and Mr. Crane lost a whole box of cold cream !   Next day we went on to Douglas, on the Border, and crossed over to Mexico to eat hot tamales.   What fun it all was !   I was sorry when the tour came to an end in San Diego, a few weeks earlier than was expected. Business had not been good, and in spite of fine notices and general enthusiasm "The Happy Stranger" (as the play was now called) did not bring in enough money to pay expenses.

I think it was while playing Santa Ana that a gentleman sent back word he wished to see me after the performance, on business. He was a representative of the Alcazar Stock Theatre in San Francisco, and had been sent to negotiate for my services in stock as leading lady to Richard Bennett for a special six weeks' engagement, opening in early June with "The Cinderella Man." I told him I would wire my decision to San Francisco within the next few days. I did not want to accept without talking it over with Mother, and then I wanted to find out when rehearsals of "The Daisy" would begin. I wired Mr. Leftvitch and received an immediate reply advising me to take the stock offer, as work would not begin on "The Daisy" before the latter part of August. Mother agreed with me that the stock experience would do me good, and the offer was financially inviting. We might as well spend the summer there as anywhere else, and the more work I had the better I liked it.

After resting in Pasadena, we set off once more for San Francisco. Rehearsals started almost immediately on "The Cinderella Man." I was very familiar with the play, having seen it many times in New York, where Phoebe Foster made such a success of the part I was now to undertake. It was difficult for me to work on material in which I so clearly remembered another person's playing. I had greatly admired Phoebe Foster in the play ; she was indeed charming, and I felt dubious of my ability to handle the part. I was tremendously helped by Richard Bennett, who besides playing the lead directed the play. He was such a splendid actor ; it seemed there was nothing he didn't know about the Theatre. I am convinced that a director who has himself a practical knowledge of acting can be of far greater help, at least to the individual performances, than one who has never actually had the experience of playing. This might be disputed in the case of great spectacles or pageants, work in which the ultimate effect is achieved through the related movement of crowd-masses ; but in handling the more intimate forms of the drama, where the ensemble is made up of delicately attuned individual characterizations, there seems no doubt of the superiority of a director intimately familiar with the actual processes of acting. Of course this in itself would not be sufficient, but, added to a natural gift for directing, it must prove invaluable.

Bennett was extremely truthful about work. He could sometimes be abominably rude, but from a technical standpoint he was invariably right, and that after all was the only thing that mattered. He instantly pounced on a couple of bad potential mannerisms in my playing and ridiculed them mercilessly. I had a bad habit of emphasizing certain points in my lines by nodding my head, or making staccato movements with my right hand. He practically tortured me out of these annoying faults. At

times we nearly came to blows, but in the end I was grateful to him.   He was charming in "The Cinderella Man,"
and when he liked could be marvelous to act with.   He
had an unerring sense of rhythm, was straightforward and
true in his playing, and directed his effects with masterly
technique.   He was a tireless worker and I never saw
him give a careless performance.

He had one very bad habit which he could not or
would not control ; he lost his temper quite obviously
on the stage if his audience did anything that annoyed
him.   I remember, once at a matinée, two ladies whisper-
ing in the front row ; he glared at them several times,
and, when that had no effect, he swore at them under his
breath just loud enough for them to hear.   They rose in
dignified horror and left the theatre, much to Bennett's
diabolical glee and the management's disapproval !

Our next production was "Rio Grande," a play by
Augustus Thomas, and the author himself came to direct
the performance.   I felt unequal to the part, for which
I was too immature, and disliked the play.   Also Mr.
Thomas's method of directing made me intensely uncomfortable.   It may have been admirable, but I found it
very difficult to adapt myself to it.   He sat out front
from the very first rehearsal with a small megaphone,
through which he shouted his instructions.   He stopped
the actors at almost every word, every movement.   They
were as puppets in his hands and had to follow meticu-
lously each inflection and execute each tiny gesture in
obedience to Mr. Thomas's conception.   This resulted

in a smooth, perfectly timed, clock-work performance, but one totally devoid, it seemed to me, of enthusiasm, glamour, or life of any kind. However, it was interesting to work under such an entirely different method.

Our next and final production was "Pierre of the Plains," a melodrama of the most lurid kind which I found hard to take seriously and in which I gave a shockingly bad performance. I remember making an entrance in the second act to slow music, covered with Fuller's earth, supposedly having ridden all night to save my sweetheart's honor, by delivering "the papers" for him, while he lay drugged by the villain, unable to perform his duty. William Boyd played my drugged sweetheart, while Bennett played the villain-hero "Pierre," a part in which he enjoyed himself hugely.

Bennett's engagement at the Alcazar had been extremely successful and the management was anxious to extend the season a few weeks. But we were very tired ; the work was terrific. We played twelve performances a week, and when we weren't playing we were rehearsing, besides which I had clothes to buy and try on. Altogether I felt ready for a breathing space before starting rehearsals of "The Daisy," of which I never ceased to dream.

Immediately on our return to New York, I reported to Mr. Leftvitch. I learned to my dismay that the project had fallen through, for financial reasons I believe. To everyone's sorrow "The Daisy" was abandoned. Such are the ways of the Theatre !

It was a sad blow ; apart from the practical end of things, it was the first play I had been connected with that had interested me deeply from an artistic angle. I never dreamed that "The Daisy" was to cross my path again several years later, when I would be better equipped to play Julie, to whom I bade a sorrowful farewell at this time.

VII

I HAD been away from New York so long that I scarcely knew where to turn to look for work. Having felt so certain of "The Daisy's" going into production, I had not even kept in touch by letter with managers or agents. By this time I should have learned never to feel certain of *anything* connected with the Theatre ! But I was still young and ignorant.

I was forced back again into small parts. A play produced by Winthrop Ames, "Saturday to Monday," had a short run. Then Faversham gave me a bit in his all-star revival of "Lord and Lady Algy."

The cast included some splendid actors: Faversham, Maxine Elliott, Irene Fenwick, Lunsden Hare, Macklyn Arbuckle, Philip Leigh, and many others. It was an interesting engagement from that angle. There was much to watch and learn.

I loved Maxine Elliott. She used to take me to lunch now and then between rehearsals, always to Child's, her "favorite restaurant." There she would sit eating corned beef hash, all unconscious of the many eyes focussed on her in amazed admiration ; she was so beautiful it was almost unbelievable. She often advised me against be-

coming a great beauty (she needn't have worried!) — it
was such an "awful nuisance," she said ! And indeed I
have often thought that unusually beautiful women must
suffer two deaths, the first immeasurably harder to bear
than the last.

Among the supers in the ballroom scene of "Lord and
Lady Algy" was a young girl, Mary Duggett, then a student at Sargent's School. We struck up a friendship that
has lasted through the years. As Mary Duggett Benson she
is now business manager of the Civic Repertory Theatre.

My lucky star had not abandoned me for good ; Miss
Ethel Barrymore came to see a performance of "Lord and
Lady Algy" and recognized in me the girl whose work
she had liked in "Mr. Lazarus." She needed an ingenue
in her next production "The Off Chance," and asked
Favvy to release me. This he was delighted to do, knowing that it would be an important step forward for me
to play a good part in Miss Barrymore's supporting cast.
She was then appearing at the Empire Theatre in a series
of productions, the current one being Edward Sheldon's
version of "The Lady of the Camelias." Ethel Barrymore was a beautiful and glamorous Marguerite Gautier ; the play was staged in the period of the book, about
1842. I have rarely seen a more hauntingly lovely
picture than Miss Barrymore, seated at the spinet at
the rise of the curtain, playing and singing "Plaisir
d'Amour." It cast a romantic dream-quality over the entire performance, and the audience sat spellbound and
deeply moved. We were rehearsing "The Off Chance"

in the daytime, and in the evenings I was allowed to slip into the stage-box to watch Miss Barrymore's Marguerite. I saw it many times and was always reduced to tears.

It is impossible to overestimate the advantage to young players of working at the side of the great ones of their profession. Unconsciously rather than consciously you absorb the best elements in acting. The whole theatre is imbued with the psychic force of a great actor, and the atmosphere becomes curiously charged with a compelling vitality. Nothing can be careless, uninteresting, or humdrum in such surroundings. No matter how big or how small the part you are playing, be it only a few lines or even a walk-on, it becomes an exciting event, and must be executed with infinite, painstaking care, for it is a part of the magical structure in which the great actor moves and has being.

The two seasons I spent in support of Miss Barrymore were of immense importance in the development of my work. There is no reason for me to speak of Ethel Barrymore as an actress ; everyone knows and loves her as a great artist ; but only those who have been privileged to work with her in the Theatre know what a really "grand" person she is. Underneath any moodiness or occasional temperamental fireworks, she has a warmth and a generosity of spirit which compel undying devotion in anyone who has ever known her. She is one of the few stars nowadays who still inspire their companies with an almost fanatical loyalty.

We played at the Empire Theatre until the end of the

season. "The Off Chance" was very successful. In it
I played Miss Barrymore's daughter, the Duchess of Bur-
chester. I had to wear very elegant clothes and much
jewelry and to my amazement was considered "radiantly
beautiful" by the critics. This impression was con-
veyed by dint of much attention to make-up and the
services of an expert hairdresser! Mother was delighted. She had thought I would spend all my life in
character rôles, more or less drab as to looks and dress,
and was much relieved to find that I could be made to
look presentable when the occasion demanded!

"The Off Chance" was followed by "Belinda," a charming trifle by A. A. Milne, in which I was again daughter
to Miss Barrymore, who gave a delicious, scintillating
performance in the title rôle.

Miss Barrymore's season was under the management
of the Frohman Company, the director of which at that
time was Alf Hayman, known among actors as one of
the grumpiest and most disagreeable of theatrical managers. When the New York season came to a close and
the time came to pay him the customary visit of thanks
for the engagement and sign a further contract if such
was contemplated, I vowed to the company that I would
succeed in shaking Mr. Hayman by the hand. They all
laughed and said such a thing had never been known to
be accomplished by a mere actor.

I knocked timidly on Alf Hayman's door and, in response to the growl that meant "Come in," entered his
large office. He was seated at his desk with a cigar be-

tween his teeth and his feet on the table. He growled a
greeting. It did not look promising ! I signed the contract for the following season, which he pushed towards
me muttering that I wasn't worth half the money and
he couldn't see why "Ethel" wanted me in the company.
I rose to go and stretched out my hand to him across the
desk, at the same time expressing my appreciation for the
season's work. He looked at my hand a moment, so surprised that his cigar almost fell from his lips ; then he
looked at me and a twinkle came into his eyes and something like a grin came over his face ; he put his cigar
down, took his feet off the table and getting up, took my
hand in a mighty grip and, with a growl that somehow
sounded friendly, shoved me out of the room. From
that day on I always liked him ; I went downstairs feeling I had achieved the distinction of shaking hands with
a polar bear !

The tour started in September ; the season was a long
one and we traveled all over the country. It was a wonderful experience. My one great difficulty was keeping
my clothes in a really Duchess-y condition, for of course
I had no maid and the management was very stingy about
cleaning bills. My second-act dress was a rose-colored
brocade and had quite a long train which was the bane
of my life. It was almost impossible to keep it clean, for
many of the stages were in a filthy condition, which the
gum-chewing habit among stage hands did nothing to
improve ! Before opening nights on the week-stands I
used to dip the offending train in a bucket of gasoline in

order to improve its complexion. In Kansas City I suffered the dreadful humiliation of receiving a letter from someone in the audience complaining bitterly that though he had never seen a real duchess, he felt sure that the state of my second-act dress, particularly *the train,* was not at all in character, and admonished me in no very polite terms to be more careful of my appearance! I was dreadfully upset, and Miss Barrymore, seeing my tear-stained face, drew from me the whole miserable story! She roared with laughter and comforted me by immediately giving orders that a new dress be sent from New York.

I shall never forget our opening in St. Louis. One of the most important actors in the play, who took the part of a western American millionaire, was found to be missing fifteen minutes before the rise of the curtain. His absence had not been noticed before, as we had arrived in town just in time for the performance, and all had been rush and bustle. He had missed his train in Chicago! The house was completely sold out and Miss Barrymore was particularly anxious for the play to go well, since St. Louis is an important town. There was no understudy. It was finally decided that the stage manager should read the part from the manuscript. An announcement was made to the house and the curtain went up. Miss Barrymore gave a superb performance, though how she ever did it I don't know. The stage manager spoke in *broad cockney,* and the effect of this accent on the slang spoken by the western millionaire was comical in the extreme. I shall always remember Miss Barrymore's face when she heard the poor man's first line ; but she continued the scene without a flicker, and it was only afterwards when the evening had been saved and the play enthusiastically received that she gave way to the laughter that had been struggling to break through.

So the weeks flew by, and finally to everyone's sorrow the tour came to an end. By June I was back in New York and once more set out on the search for work.

June is not a good time to find work in New York. It is too late for try-outs or stock engagements and too early for legitimate productions.

Mother had decided, now that I was fairly established in my work in America, to go back to Europe to live and, having always loved England above any other country, she made her home in London. I was therefore alone in New York and felt that for the summer the Hotel Algonquin would be a good centre. I would be in touch there with the activities of the Theatre, and I was anxious to work as soon as possible. It had not been easy with my responsibilities, which naturally grew with my age, to save money on the salary then at my command, and the summer was a lean one. I lived in a small back room at the Algonquin and took most of my meals out, most often at the Russian Inn on Thirty-seventh Street, run by a charming woman, Ray Davidson Rosenbaum, a sister of the great sculptor Jo Davidson. Often when I had no money she fed me for nothing, as she did many

other young artists.   She was a kindly, cultured, warm-
hearted Russian woman ; her generosity was really her
undoing.   She could never refuse food or money to an
artist in need.   At this time I was deep in the study of
Russian ; for months I had been learning this fascinating
language out of books and dictionaries.   My great dream
was to read Tchekov in the original, for I had become
obsessed by his plays.   I felt that not having the small-
est key to Tchekov's real language would be a great
handicap to some day translating the spirit of his work.
There, in the little restaurant on Thirty-seventh Street,
I tried to put into practice the archaic book-knowledge
acquired with so much application.   Ray Davidson was
(and still is) an indefatigable idealist.   She is a great
lover of fine literature, especially Russian, and worked
with me for hours on Pushkin and Lermontov, trying to
instill in me a feeling for the rhythmical beauty and
richness of this extraordinary language.

While looking for serious work in the Theatre, I
would occasionally land a job as super in a movie for ten
dollars a day, and thus managed to eke out the summer.
I finally found a play in which I was interested and in which
my services were required — a difficult combination !   It
was a play called "Lusmore," founded upon an old Irish
legend, and I was to take the part of the blind girl Eithne.
The play was the work of Grace Heyer, who took the
part of the youth "Lusmore."   It was really an Irish
fairy tale, too full of lyric imagination to be a lasting

draw on Broadway.   Mrs. Chauncey Olcott was manager
and co-author.   It was a beautiful opportunity for me ;
the part of Eithne was a grateful one, but the play was
not robust enough to last, and in a month it went the
way of all failures and I was once more jobless.

At this time Elsie Janis was planning to present her
first "Gang Show" — "Elsie Janis and her Gang" — and,
knowing I was out of work, she invited me to join the
"gang" as the French girl and also as her dancing part-
ner in a scene in which she took the part of a *Chasseur
Alpin.*   I wasn't worried about my French, but I was
worried about my dancing.   However, Elsie took me in
hand and I swear she could make anything in this world
dance !   I spoke nothing but French in my scenes (that
was easy !) but Elsie literally *made* me dance.   We had a
sort of potpourri number in which we started with a fox-
trot working into a tango ; then a waltz working into a
finale Castle Walk.   How Elsie made me do it I don't
know, but she did !   We used to get an encore at every
show.

During these rehearsals I realized the agility of Elsie's
brain.   We used to work in a big hall somewhere uptown, and I have often seen her direct in one corner of
the hall a sketch, in another corner a specialty dance,
while in another corner she would try to initiate me into
the mystery of "turns."   In the meantime she would be
jotting something down on a piece of paper.   At the
end of an hour the sketch, the specialty, and the turns

would be pretty well set, and she would produce on the piece of paper a corking set of lyrics for the composer's latest tune.   What a worker !

It was great fun, this experience in musical comedy — so different from anything I had been accustomed to. We played at the George M. Cohan Theatre.   The show was a great success, but I had to ask for a release, for I had been offered the leading part in a play by Ian Hay Beith, "Tilly of Bloomsbury."   Elsie well knew that my first and only love was the so-called "legitimate theatre," and of course didn't want to stand in my way.

"Tilly of Bloomsbury," a great London success, was to be produced in this country by Al Woods.   I had been told that the leading part of Tilly was a great catch.   It was one of those deceptive "leading lady" parts that are really bad ; but I didn't know enough in those days to realize that, and was unreservedly happy at my good fortune.   There was to be a try-out for a couple of weeks ; the tour included Montreal and Washington.   I became great friends with the author, Ian Hay, one of the finest and most delightful men I have ever known. He liked my performance and gave me every encouragement.   The opening in Montreal was promising and I enjoyed the engagement, though I was puzzled by the part which was (according to all that I had been told) a "great" one ; for try as I would to play it with every ounce of enthusiasm, sincerity, and vigor I had in me, it was always swamped by the strong comedy element in the play.

It was during this try-out engagement that I met for the second time a darling old character actor, George Giddons. We had played together in "The Melody of Youth." In "Tilly of Bloomsbury" he gave a poignant and beautiful performance. He was a very old man, I think in his eighties, and though hale and hearty would quite easily drop into a doze during his waits off-stage. I soon got on to this and made it my business (keeping in mind my experience with dear Mr. Crane) to watch him before an entrance cue. He would be sound asleep in a chair in the wings, and about a minute before his entrance I would quite casually wake him up. He never knew I did it purposely! He would rise to his feet, stand at his entrance in readiness, and appear on the stage with more vitality and enthusiasm than most young men of twenty could summon up. What a beautiful actor he was, so simple and sincere and with such unerring technique!

We opened in Washington at Poli's Theatre. The play received good notices, but I felt deathly ill. I had caught a bad attack of influenza, of which an epidemic was raging, and had to give up after the second performance. I think Al Woods intended firing me anyhow, and my illness gave him a good excuse. He was generous and kind as ever, and in spite of giving me my notice softened the blow by paying my doctor's bills and my expenses while I was ill for three weeks with pneumonia in a Washington hotel.

I don't know how I should ever have managed to get

home without Ian Hay.   He came all the way to Washington to fetch me, arranged for a wheelchair at the station and a drawing-room on the train, and on reaching New York took me home and carried me up four flights of stairs to my apartment.   I was so weak I could scarcely stand on my feet, and the stairs made it very difficult for me to go out for some time.

I had been in New York a couple of weeks when Mr. Caryl of the Shubert office telephoned and told me he had the "cutest ingenue part" he wanted to try me in.   I still felt weak and ill, and no "cute ingenue" was going to lure me out of my hole ; I didn't feel either "cute" or in an ingenue mood !   I told him I was sorry but I was not yet strong enough to start work and thanked him for his thought of me.

Two more weeks went by ; again Mr. Caryl on the telephone presenting glowing accounts of his "cute ingenue."   He was very upset, for the play was to open in two weeks and the part was still uncast ; they could not seem to find the right actress.   I answered as before. "No cute ingenues for me !" thought I.

He finally persuaded me to read the play at least, and to this I consented ; he sent it over to me by special messenger.   I was so completely uninterested in all he had told me of the part that I could scarcely bring myself to look at the manuscript.   However, I had promised to read it, and read it I must.   I saw that the play was called "Not So Long Ago" and written by someone of the name of Arthur Richman, that it took place in

New York in the seventies, and that the "cute ingenue" was named Elsie Dover. I started to read. I could scarcely believe my eyes ; was *this* the play Mr. Caryl had described to me ? Was *this* the "cute ingenue part" he had so insistently referred to ? I read on to the end in breathless excitement. The play was a delightful, whimsical comedy, and the part of Elsie Dover one of the best character-comedy rôles I had come across. There was nothing in the least "cute" about her ! She was a living human being, full of amusing and unexpected quirks, somewhat like a Barrie creation. I *must* play her ! I instinctively felt it would be a turning point in my career if I did. I was now filled with terror lest Mr. Caryl had found someone else in the meantime and I had missed my chance. I flung on my clothes and descended the stairs as fast as my still wobbly legs would carry me.

Mr. Caryl was in his office, and I greeted him with the cry : "Why did you keep telling me it was a 'cute ingenue' ? It's a splendid part, and I must play it !" I then explained to him that I was dreadfully weak and begged to be allowed to rehearse sitting down as much as possible, and also begged to be left to my own instinct as far as playing the part was concerned ; there were only ten days left for rehearsals before the try-out opened in Washington, and I assured him that if he would trust me and leave me alone I could play the part.

All this was agreed on ; I signed my contract and started work the next morning. Mr. Caryl was as good

as his word ; I was left to my own devices and enjoyed
for the first time the privilege of working a part out in
exactly my own way.

I have since discovered, through my own directing
experience, that there are two distinct types of players :
those who work slowly from inside out, gradually shaping
their parts to conform with a definite inner conception ;
and those who work from outside in, who build up their
characterizations with the help of externals only, until
the proper mood is created within them. There are
great actors among both types (and plenty of bad ones
too !). It is just that their creative methods are dia-
metrically opposed. I have always found in dealing
with the first type (to which I belong) that the wisest policy is to leave them alone at least for the first couple of
weeks, until they have fairly well sketched in their canvas, and then help them mostly through suggestion, seldom through meticulous detailed direction, which is apt
to blur the clarity of their own conception and make
their performance lifeless and mechanical. The second
group, on the other hand, welcome detailed, elaborate
direction from the start and indeed feel lost without it.
Most directors fail to make this important distinction ;
they are generally too prone to treat all actors alike.

The play went splendidly at the try-out, but there were
a few changes to be made in the text and in the cast, so
we closed for a couple of weeks of additional rehearsals.
I was terrified of being fired ; this time I felt I simply
couldn't have borne it ! For although my notices had

been wonderful I had at last learned never to be certain
of anything in the Theatre until it has actually taken
place. I thought I should feel sure of really playing
the part after the curtain had dropped on the New York
first night, and not before !

A second try-out followed ; we played Boston for a
couple of weeks. Sydney Blackmer, the leading man,
was delightful in the part of Billie Ballard. We were
both highly praised, and I received my first really important notice in the *Boston Evening Transcript,* from
Mr. H. T. Parker. It was important to me because it
did not just indiscriminately laud me to the skies. It
showed me that Mr. Parker had watched my work carefully for several years, had noted the development in it,
and had been on the alert for any bad habits that might
creep into it, one or two of which he warned me against.
It showed, too, a real knowledge of the art of acting, a
realization of the facts that this difficult art cannot be
learned in five minutes and that a child of twenty should
not be expected to give the performance of a woman of
thirty-five, nor should she be extravagantly praised into
believing she has nothing more to learn. His feeling
was that I had very unusual talent and with many years
of hard work might turn into a fine actress.

I was tremendously grateful to Mr. Parker for the wise
and helpful tone of his notice, and since then I have had
many an interesting review to thank him for ; he does
not always agree with my conception of a part, but at
least he pays me the compliment of seeing that I have

one, and that my performance did not just "happen that way" by accident !

The New York opening of "Not So Long Ago" was a great event in my life. That night, like Alice in "Through the Looking Glass," I moved into another "square." It was tremendously exciting. Blackmer and I were recalled again and again ; we were certainly two happy children that evening ! The play was an instantaneous hit, and in spite of the warm weather ran all through the summer at the Booth Theatre to crowded houses. The greatest proof that Sydney Blackmer and I had that we really and truly had made good in no mean fashion, was the appearance backstage after the second performance of Mr. Caryl, bearing two long-term contracts which Mr. Shubert was anxious to have us sign. They were for three years with an option for a year more. They were by no means brilliant as far as salaries went, but Sydney and I felt so grateful to the management that had "discovered" us that we signed without hesitation. We were unwise children as well as happy ones !

VIII

AFTER basking in success and prosperity for several months, scarcely able to believe my good fortune, I gradually grew restless.   It was then that the disadvantage of the long-run system for young players, who should be constantly at work developing the different sides of their talent, was forcibly borne in on me.   I knew that playing the same part night after night, no matter how conscientiously, was not enough ; but where could one go, what could one do, to gain additional training and experience ?

Mary Kennedy (who played a charming comedy part in "Not So Long Ago") and I discussed the situation and finally hit upon an idea which we believed might be practical.   Our plan was to get together all the successful young players who felt as we did the stultifying influence of the long-run system and were anxious for added work ; we would organize an association, and work on some of the great plays of the world, simply for the joy of the work itself, without any thought of performing them publicly.   In this way we would be able to tackle parts which we were not yet experienced enough to undertake openly.   The plays would be chosen by a majority vote

145

and it would be arranged that each member in turn had a chance at a leading part while the rest of us formed the supporting company.

I wrote to several great actors and actresses asking them to be on a committee, which we hoped might help us with advice and criticism. I received very encouraging response, Mrs. Fiske being particularly interested in the scheme. The young actors we approached were all enthusiastic ; Margalo Gillmore, Henry Hull, Phoebe Foster, Katherine Cornell, and Tom Powers are some that come to my mind.

Mary Kennedy and I thought of nothing else and worked at the plan with fanatical energy. Unfortunately she discussed the scheme with two young men, whose names I have forgotten, who instantly saw the practical and even commercial potentialities in the idea. Mary was taken in by their enthusiasm, thinking it sprang from the same source as our own, and persuaded me to take them into a kind of partnership. When I realized that their ideas included Sunday performances with all-star casts of young well-known players, at which they naturally figured much money could be taken in, I saw that our initial plan was being pushed aside, and I washed my hands of the whole business. I think in the end nothing came of it ; but I was bitterly disappointed and hurt. Naturally, as soon as public performances entered into the matter, the whole freedom to work experimentally was lost. What I had dreamed of creating was a workshop where, untroubled by outside opinion, we could improve and perfect our instruments.

When the long New York run came to an end we spent a whole season on the road. The tour took us all over the country and was everywhere very successful. During this tour I struck up a great and enthusiastic friendship with Thomas Mitchell who played the comic-villain, Sam. I had never seen much of him in New York, away from the Theatre, but on the road we suddenly discovered each other and were practically inseparable.

We were both overbearingly ambitious and both had idealistic dreams for the Theatre. We decided that one day we would manage our own company, and we started choosing the plays. These included, I remember distinctly, "The Master Builder," "L'Aiglon," and "Savva" by Andreyev, in which it was Tommy's great longing to play. I was working very hard at a translation of "L'Aiglon," for none of the published ones satisfied me ! We often sat up all night in hotel lobbies and lunch-wagons reading the latest pages of my "L'Aiglon" version, or having frantic arguments about "The Master Builder" — a subject, by the way, which I recommend to those fond of arguments as inexhaustible !

I hadn't seen Tommy Mitchell for ten years when we met a few weeks ago after his performance of "Riddle Me This," and we started right in again on "The Master Builder" as though we had only just left off the night before. We kept it up till five in the morning, much to the amazement of the other occupants of the speak-easy in which we found ourselves, to whom Ibsen was just "Ibsen" and "The Master Builder" some sort of patent construction material !

At the close of the tour I asked Mr. Shubert for a few weeks' breathing space before starting on another play. He had not yet decided on anything for me and I was most anxious to know what my fate would be. In the meantime I decided on a real rest and set off by myself on a trip to the Coast by way of the Grand Canyon, where I spent several days. I wanted to be quite alone and, in order to cut myself right off, purposely told no one where I was going, and left no address of any kind.

I was away about six weeks and on my return to New York met a girl on the street who had played with me in "Lusmore." She told me she had just come from the Theatre Guild office, where she went in search of a job, and had heard that the directors had been trying to get in touch with me everywhere. She thought it was in connection with the leading part in "Liliom," which was to go into immediate rehearsal with the young German actor Joseph Schildkraut in the title rôle. Mr. Shubert had not yet decided on a play for me, and, realizing that anything produced by the Theatre Guild might prove interesting, I went directly down to their offices in the old Garrick Theatre.

I was greeted with open arms ; they wanted me for "Liliom" ; young Schildkraut had said I was the only actress he wanted to play it with. I had met him once,

while playing in "Not So Long Ago" at the Booth Theatre. After a matinée he had rushed backstage in his
usual whirlwind fashion and had almost bowled me over
with his enthusiasm over my work, which was expressed
with all that colossal vitality of which he is the enviable
possessor. It had apparently not been idle praise, for
here he was insisting that I play opposite him in "Liliom"
and would hear of nothing else. I asked to read the
manuscript and walked home with it under my arm.

I knew nothing about the play except that it was translated from the Hungarian and the name of the author
was Molnar. I was surprised on opening the manuscript to see that the name of my part was "Julie," but
thought it merely a coincidence until I started to read
the play. Was it possible? I thought I had taken leave
of my senses! But no — it was true! The play was
"The Daisy" and Julie was *my* Julie, to whom I had bade
a sorrowful farewell four years before. This was a different adaptation, keeping close to the original in title
and locale. Of course there was no doubt in my mind
that I must play it, and I set off to get Mr. Shubert's permission. He consented to lend me to the Guild until
he should find a suitable play for me, and the next morning I started rehearsals at the Garrick Theatre.

My first day of work on "Liliom" was not a happy one.
The rehearsal was called for eleven o'clock and when the
break for lunch was announced a little after one, I went
to Miss Helburn's office and in no uncertain terms in-

formed her it would unfortunately be impossible for me to attempt the part under Mr. Reicher's direction. He seemed to consider me an insensitive fool, and I simply could not work with anyone holding such an opinion.

Miss Helburn behaved with remarkable patience, and instead of boxing my ears or giving me a good spanking, invited me to have a bite of lunch at her club. During lunch she begged me to try again. She promised to speak to Frank Reicher and tell him to leave me strictly alone for the first couple of weeks.

This he certainly did, in a very pointed manner, for he was rightly angry at what he considered my ridiculous exhibition of temperament.

It was not until the third week of rehearsals that we started to notice one another ; he had been pleased with the way I was developing my part and, watching him work, I had realized that he was an unusually fine director. I felt I had been an idiot, decided to make peace overtures, which were gladly accepted, and we became the best of friends. He helped me greatly with my performance, showing me how to build up and project clearly a point which I was but faintly indicating, the value of a longer pause here or the danger of too long a one somewhere else. Having watched me for two weeks or more in silence, he had clearly grasped the best way to handle me, and guided me gently and understandingly towards the final interpretation.

To everyone's amazement "Liliom" was a colossal popular "hit." An artistic success had been counted on, but no one had dreamed the play would be a big box-office draw. Schildkraut played superbly the opening night, while I, on the contrary, gave one of the worst performances of my life. To me it was an evening of utter misery. I knew I was playing badly and somehow just couldn't stop. I was so nervous that my mouth was parched and dry. I was tied up in a thousand knots, and no emotion would come into my despairing soul. I felt as though I were in a straitjacket, and struggle as I might, could not break free. It was a nightmare. After the performance I would see no one and fled from the theatre consumed with shame and anguish. I remember crying all night. To my amazement the next morning the telephone never stopped ringing; congratulations poured in; I was told that the notices were magnificent, that the show was a "knock-out," and that I must be the happiest girl in the world!

We moved to a larger theatre, the Fulton. The success of the play was phenomenal. A couple of months after the opening I was horrified by a message from the Shubert office informing me that Mr. Shubert wanted me to leave "Liliom" and intended using me in an English play called "The Blue Lagoon." I read the play and was disgusted with it; it seemed to me awful trash and I felt sure that it wouldn't stand a chance. In any case I couldn't bear the thought of giving up Julie, and certainly not for "The Blue Lagoon." I rushed over to see Mr. Shubert, determined to persuade him to give up his plan. I remembered some advice Mr. Belasco had given me a year or two before ; he assured me that the two things no manager could withstand were floods of tears and hysterics.   I made up my mind to use both on poor "Mr. Lee."   My scheme worked : Mr. Shubert gave in !   I left the office relieved and grateful.

"Liliom" ran all through the summer and the following winter.   I was once more seized with a restless desire for more work.   Arthur Row conceived the idea of an "Afternoon Theatre," which would present unusual and little-known plays for special matinées ; this plan permitted actors in long-run engagements to take part in these performances.   He had chosen Maeterlinck's "Aglavaine and Sélysette" to inaugurate his scheme.   Clare Eames was to be Aglavaine and Mr. Row asked me to play Sélysette.   It is a beautiful but extremely difficult play.   The part of Sélysette appealed to me tremendously, however, and I was only too glad to accept Mr. Row's offer.

I was much interested in Clare Eames ; at first I couldn't make out whether she was one of the worst actresses I'd ever seen or whether she was a genius ; her work was bewilderingly uneven ; the intensity and even violence of her temperament made moderation impossible ; there was no middle path ; in one scene she would be unbelievably bad and in the next superb.   She was an indefatigable worker and one of the most uncompromising artists I've ever known.   Later years proved her unmistakable genius ; had she lived I am convinced she would have been the greatest actress of our time ;

her death was a shocking and irreparable loss to the American Theatre.

The performance of "Aglavaine and Sélysette" was not a good one. I was completely out of my depth, and played in an indefinite, colorless manner. Where Clare Eames *over*stressed, I *under*stressed ; there was no cohesion in our work together ; we had started at different ends of the scale. The play itself could, of course, never have a very general appeal, but it was received with interest by a small minority of ardent theatre-lovers, and we repeated it at a second matinée.

I always felt Mr. Arthur Row's idea was a good one ; it is too bad he was not given the financial support necessary to continue his experiment ; but in this country it is extremely difficult to raise money for the Theatre, at least for idealistic purposes.

At the end of the New York run the Shuberts took over "Liliom" for the road, and in late spring we started off. It was planned to play through the summer in Chicago. We opened there, and I suddenly had a complete nervous collapse and had to stop acting. The part of Julie is a very trying one ; it is highly emotional, but the emotion is for the most part repressed ; the whole character is in a melancholy minor strain. The repetition for over a year, night after night, of Julie's complete and unexpressed anguish became too much for my nerves. I had begged Mr. Shubert to give us a short break during the summer, but I suppose he thought I was just lazy and paid no attention to my repeated request ! I warned him my doctor had predicted a crash, and sure enough it came. I was sent back to New York, where I remained in bed for two or three weeks ; a trip to Europe was recommended, and as soon as I had recovered sufficient strength I sailed on the *Mauretania*.

AMONG the many passengers on board were Miss Elsie Ferguson and Mr. and Mrs. George Arliss. Miss Ferguson was kindness itself to me. Seeing I was traveling alone and was obviously in a weak and painfully nervous condition, she took pity on me and insisted on my taking meals at her table and sitting with her on deck. If it hadn't been for her gracious care I don't think I should have summoned up enough courage to leave my cabin. I was morbidly sensitive at this time and terrified of people. It has taken me years to overcome this ridiculous and torturing shyness. To walk into a crowded room was agony ; to talk to a stranger almost an impossibility. People thought me rude and very conceited ; if they could only have known the shrinking timidity that had taken possession of my entire being !

It was seven years since I had seen Europe. It seemed incredible. So many things had happened in those years ; I was grown up now and in many ways tremendously changed. How tiny everything looked ! How charming ! How ridiculously touching ! I stood on the deck with the tears pouring down my face ; the old colors, the old shapes, the old smells and sounds, how friendly and soothing they seemed. "Old Nurse Eu-

(*Above*) "The Off Chance"   (*Below*) "Not So Long Ago"

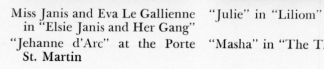

Miss Janis and Eva Le Gallienne   "Julie" in "Liliom"
in "Elsie Janis and Her Gang"
"Jehanne d'Arc" at the Porte   "Masha" in "The Three Sisters"
St. Martin

rope !" I thought, and with a sigh of comfort gave myself
up to her healing touch.   And yet I felt definitely a part
of America ; I did not want to live anywhere else, certainly not to *work* anywhere else ; but I was sick and
dreadfully tired and could think of nothing but rest.

I went straight to London to stay with Mother.   A few
weeks later we went to Paris.   Nothing had changed ;
every tree, every stone was familiar and full of memories.
I spent days wandering about the Luxembourg ; Mme.
Coudret and Thérèse still led their goat- and donkey-
carts laden with children round the bassin ; the same
man hired out the same old boats ; the guards, the
balloon-lady, the chair lady were all the same.   Only
Mme. Kapelaer had gone, and another face looked out
at me from her old booth.   "Yes, Mme. Kapelaer died
about a year ago, Mademoiselle," I was told.   I missed
her ; she and her *caoutchoucs* had been so much a part
of my childhood.

Later in the summer I went to Vienna and on to Budapest.   I was anxious to meet Molnar and see the town
which was the scene of "Liliom."   It was a fascinating
visit.   I reached Budapest in the evening and went to
the Dunapalota, where they gave me a room with a balcony looking out over the beautiful Danube.   The next
morning about seven o'clock I was awakened by a furious knocking at the door.   I spoke no Magyar and my
German was nothing to boast about, but I heard several
voices repeating the word "fotograf," and opening the
door was faced by several gentlemen with cameras and

several ladies with notebooks. They had discovered that
I had played "Julie" in America and wanted pictures
and interviews. I struggled into some clothes and was
snapped many times on the balcony, while the ladies
interviewed me, a difficult procedure on account of language, but we managed somehow.

On my last day in Budapest Molnar gave a lunch in
my honor. We sat down to table at noon and the meal
lasted till nearly six. I was the only woman there ; the
other guests were all well-known artists, writers, painters,
and directors. I carried on a difficult conversation in
many languages. Molnar spoke French, one or two
spoke English, the rest German, one Danish, and one
could speak only Magyar and a little Russian ! It was
quite a struggle to keep up, but it was great fun, though
very tiring.

Molnar then insisted on taking me out to the Amusement Park which was "Liliom's" real background. We
drove off in a little open victoria drawn by two horses
and spent a couple of hours surrounded by merry-go-
rounds, swings, and Punch and Judy shows. Molnar
and I had our picture taken together in the photogra-
pher's booth that had served as a model for the second
and third acts of Liliom : "The lady looks at the gentleman and the gentleman looks straight into the camera !"

At last I felt it was time to return to the hotel. I
was leaving by plane for Paris at five-thirty the next
morning, and I had not yet packed my bags. But Molnar would not hear of my leaving the party ; I must

stay with them until time for the plane to leave ; they would all come with me and see me off.

They returned with me to the hotel while I packed my few belongings and then took me to a theatre where "Le Chasseur de chez Maxim" was being played in Magyar. Unfortunately it was the "off" season in the theatres, and the best actors were all in the country having their summer's rest. I was taken backstage after the performance to meet the company, who were most kind and genial, though we could do little more than smile at each other and shake hands many times. After this we went on to an artist's club, "Fescek," where we had supper and sat talking till past four in the morning, when it was time to start for the flying field. As we left the club Molnar hailed a cab, and the old coachman, recognizing me from pictures that had appeared in the papers the day before, got down from his seat and clapping me heartily on the back exclaimed, *"So ! Sie haben in Amerika die Julika gespielt !"* I felt immensely flattered, he was so jovial and pleased with himself and with me !

Molnar was furious with me for traveling by plane. It was so dangerous ! It was ridiculous to take such unnecessary risks. He made me promise to send a telegram the moment I arrived in Paris, to let them all know I was safe. I left the whole party waving below on the flying field as the plane rose in the air and headed towards Vienna. I had had a marvelous time. Their generous warmth and eager interest in me had been exciting and stimulating, but a lunch-party that lasts from twelve

noon on one day until five-thirty A. M. the next proves
a little tiring and I sat back in the wicker armchair of
the plane, my head whirling with so many impressions,
happy but completely exhausted !

The first stop was Vienna.   Here we were unduly de-
layed by a lady who was flying to Prague.   She had an
enormous amount of luggage and one trunk that was so
large that, try as they would, they could not force it into
the cockpit.   She was very excitable and insistent.   They
even took the door off its hinges in an effort to accommodate the offending trunk, but all to no avail.   She had to
make arrangements to have it shipped by train, and, still
bewailing her fate and sobbing with hysterical annoyance, she was whisked off to Prague, where we arrived in
a couple of hours.

At Prague we changed into a larger plane bound for
Strasbourg.   We were relieved of the noisy lady, and the
only remaining passenger was a young Frenchman.   The
four hours' trip was uneventful, but to our disgust we
found that being nearly an hour behind our schedule, we
had missed the connecting plane at Strasbourg, and there
was no other leaving for Paris that evening.   There was
nothing to do but wait for the train, which would bring
us in to the Gare de l'Est around six in the morning.
The young Frenchman asked me if I would be kind
enough to dine with him ; he was a very pleasant companion and we sat at a little restaurant on the square
opposite the cathedral chatting over our coffee until
time came to go to the station, where we climbed into an

empty compartment.   Here, stretching out each on our *banquette,* we fell sound asleep and did not stir till in the gray dawn the train puffed into the Gare de l'Est.

That same day Mother and I returned to London, and a few days later I took the boat train to Southampton. I now felt eager to be home in New York again and, full of renewed energy, was anxious to get back to work.

Rehearsals of "Liliom" started at once.   There were a few changes in the cast ; we lost Hortense Alden, who gave such a wonderful performance as Marie ; we also had a new Mrs. Muskat, and a new child in the last scene. This has always been a very difficult part to cast.   We tried out at least twenty girls ; they were either too old, or too affected, or too American in type ; Schildkraut and I were in despair.   We finally discovered little Rose Hobart, then only fifteen years old ; she was a perfect type for the part and showed every promise of becoming a fine actress.   By a curious coincidence she played the part of "Julie" in the movies several years later, when the play was filmed, and with notable success.

The tour lasted all season.   Schildkraut and I were now starred in the play.   It was a strange sensation see-ing one's name in electric lights.   To my surprise I did not find it pleasant ; I had always dreamed of it and imagined it would be a "grand and glorious feeling." But the first time I looked up at the front of the house and saw "Le Gallienne" shining in bright electric bulbs, I felt so frightened I wanted to run away and hide.   It seemed so ridiculous ; I felt ashamed and unworthy.

Schildkraut had to leave the cast six weeks before the end of the tour ; he was to begin rehearsals of "Peer Gynt" which the Guild was producing with Komissar-shevsky as director. I had to carry on with Charles Ellis playing opposite me ; and although Ellis was good in the part, I missed Schildkraut, who had given such a perfect performance, and so was glad when the long season at last came to a close.

IX

By this time my contract with the Shuberts was up, and as they had no play in which I felt interested, I decided to try my luck with some other management. The great difficulty lay in the fact that I had become associated in people's minds, through my long appearance in "Liliom," with sad melancholy parts, "waifs," and "forlorn peasants." This infuriated me, and I resolved to wait until an entirely different type of character should be offered me.

In the meantime I played for a few weeks with Basil Sydney in a play by Mercedes de Acosta called "Sandro Botticelli," which was produced at the Provincetown Theatre. There were many beautiful and poetical passages in the play, which in idea and intention was very lovely, but like many first plays it did not stand up under performance ; the fabric was not tightly woven nor robust enough, and the venture was a dismal failure.

I was anxious to go to Europe again for the summer, but did not want to leave until my plans for the fall season were definitely decided. At last I got a message from Mr. Gilbert Miller's office. He was now head of the Frohman Company and was himself in Europe at the time, but had cabled his representative, Mr. Reilly, to engage me for Molnar's play "The Swan" which he planned for early fall production. I read the play and found to my delight that the part of Alexandra was that of a princess, that there was nothing of the waif or forlorn peasant about her. Feeling that she would make an excellent contrast to Julie and finding the play charming, I signed the contract with Mr. Reilly and sailed the next day for Europe.

In London I met Mr. Gilbert Miller who gave me *carte blanche* to go to Paris and buy my clothes for the play. It was Molyneux who made me the beautiful second-act dress that was so much admired. I also provided myself with ear-rings, a tiara, and fans ; it was fun to think of wearing some lovely things on the stage again after two years of poor Julie's rags.

One of the most important events in my life took place during this European visit : I saw Eleonora Duse act. I did not know very much about her ; Mother had always considered Bernhardt the greater of the two and Duse was scarcely referred to. I had discovered a photograph of her, which cast a strange spell over me and came to me at a time when I was greatly in need of help : she had written on it : *"Je vous souhaite Force et Confiance de vivre !"* and the words *"Force et Confiance"* came to me as a gift. I seized them and made them completely mine. I used to repeat to myself over and over again *"Force et Confiance, Force et Confiance,"* like a prayer. They meant so much to me that I had them engraved as a sort of crest on my note-paper and other belongings.

I had read reports, just before sailing, of Mme. Duse's return to the Theatre and of the extraordinary success she was having in London, where, under the management of Charles Cochran, she was playing two matinées a week to packed houses at the enormous Oxford Theatre. I cabled R. H. P. to get me seats for her last performance, which took place a couple of days after my arrival in England. With great difficulty he procured some tickets on the fifteenth row ; it was the best he could do.

The curtain rose on "Cosi Sia," and at the same time on a new epoch in my life. At the first sound of Duse's voice, at the first glimpse of her face, tears came into my eyes ; tears of wonder, tears of exaltation ; for the first time in this world I felt I was looking upon perfect Beauty.

Her performance was to me a revelation and at the same time a confirmation. Her playing was like the fulfillment of my vision of what playing might be ; but I had never expected to see it, and now that she is gone, none of us will ever see it again.

After the first act I got hold of Mr. Cochran and persuaded him to let me sit on the floor in the first row aisle ; I could not bear to be so far away ; although I felt the full force of Duse's playing from afar, I wanted desperately to be close to it. After the final curtain I was in a sort of daze. I lost all my belongings, hat, coat, pocketbook, everything ; my one thought was to get away from people and enjoy in the fullness of solitude the tremendous ecstasy with which her performance filled me. I had suddenly come face to face with an actress who brought the art of the Theatre on a level with the greatest sculpture, painting, music, and poetry ; who had succeeded through superhuman understanding and compassion in raising an art that is commonly looked upon as one of mere interpretation, to the sphere of metaphysical and impersonal creative genius.

I walked for hours through the London streets ; at last I returned home to a slightly irate Mother, and on the way sent some flowers to Mme. Duse with the note : *"Vous m'avez donnée force et confiance de vivre."* I knew my signature could mean nothing to her, even if she had been able to decipher it, which was problematical in view of its ever-cryptic form.

The next day I went to Paris ; there I found that Mme. Duse was staying at the Hotel Regina. There was, I heard, a possibility of her appearing in New York, but a mere possibility.   I felt that if for a moment I could be privileged to see her it would bring to me a new strength, a new faith, for which I was frantically searching.   I went to the hotel and sent her some word.   Her companion, Désirée, came to see me and informed me that Mme. Duse's New York contract was probably going through.   If such was the case, Mme. Duse would prefer to see me in New York, for she would be leaving for Switzerland the following evening and was tired and ill. She would send me word.

The next morning I received the following letter:

*"Merci pour vos bonnes paroles ; merci pour les fleurs.
Regrette aujourd'hui impossible — peut-être demain.*

E. Duse"

But *demain* she had left for Switzerland, and I had the assurance that in all probability she would be playing in New York the following winter.

A month later I was in the full swing of "The Swan" rehearsals at the Empire Theatre. The play was directed by David Burton, a sympathetic, sensitive director. The cast, as usual in a Gilbert Miller production, was exceptionally fine — the Prince, Philip Merivale ; the tutor, Basil Rathbone ; the Friar, Halliwell Hobbes ; the majordomo, Richie Ling ; the Mother, Hilda Spong ; the Dowager Princess, Alison Skipworth ; Symphorosa, Alice John.

All went well and we opened in Detroit for the first week of our try-out ; the second week we played Montreal, and our opening in New York was set for a Wednesday in October at the Cort Theatre.

In the meantime, the appearance of Mme. Duse for a series of performances opening at the Metropolitan Opera House and later for matinées at the Century Theatre under the auspices of Morris Gest had been definitely announced.

I wrote to the Gest office and reserved seats on the first row for every matinée performance, which out of consideration for the theatrical profession had been scheduled for Tuesdays and Fridays. New York owes a great debt of gratitude to Morris Gest ; it was he who

had given us an opportunity to see the Reinhardt productions, the unforgettable Moscow Art Theatre Company, and now, Eleonora Duse. A curious combination
of great showman and idealistic visionary, Gest has been
an important factor in the history of the American
Theatre.

As my opening in "The Swan" drew nearer, I became
ill with nerves. I had refused to be starred, but was suffering from the sort of pernicious suggestion often found
in the Broadway Theatre. On every side was the in-
sinuation : "If our 'little Swan' is all right, the play will
be a hit." This is enough to make one's opening night
performance bad under any circumstances.

I had been playing Montreal when the news of Mme.
Duse's arrival was announced in the papers. On my
return to New York on the Monday, I naturally wouldn't
have dreamed of disturbing her, for I knew her own
opening was in a very few days and that she would be
harassed and troubled. But on the morning of the
Wednesday, the day of "The Swan" première, I went to
her hotel, the Majestic (now torn down), and left some
flowers for her, and a letter in which I told her of my
coming ordeal that evening and begged her to pray for
me ! Just as I was leaving the desk, having deposited
my note and flowers with the clerk, Désirée stepped out
of the elevator. She at once recognized me and came
towards me. She was very kind and told me that Mme.
Duse had read in the papers of my opening in "The

"Princess Alexandra" in "The Swan"

Madame Eleanora Duse   *Photo by Arnold Genthe, N. Y.*

Swan" and was hoping I would play well. I left the hotel full of comfort, and went home and to bed, to rest until the evening.

I had not been in bed more than an hour when the doorbell rang. I answered it and there stood Désirée. She explained to me that Mme. Duse had been very angry with her for not bringing me to her at once when she met me in the hotel lobby, and said that if I felt like making the effort, Duse would be only too happy to see me before the evening's performance. In any case she had written me a letter which Désirée then handed to me. Mme. Duse wrote :

"*Chère, Belle Enfant, Chère Artiste qui est en peine pour son Art ! Je voudrais tant vous consoler — vous dire d'être sûre de vous-même. Je me gronde de ne pas venir à votre recherche — et je n'ose pas sortir de cette chambre ! Pardonnez — et soyez heureuse. 'E nella luce.'*

Eleonora Duse"

I flung on my clothes and followed Désirée. I was filled with a passionate desire to thank this great artist for the amazingly generous gesture which only *such* an artist could have conceived and put into execution.

In a half-hour I was ushered by Désirée into Mme. Duse's drawing-room. She came towards me, her hands outstretched, her beautifully worn face full of that luminous, warm expectancy which was almost childlike in its eager sincerity and faith. One of the first things she said to me was : *"Où avez-vous trouvé ces mots 'Force et Confiance' ?"* I answered : *"Mais, Mme. Duse, c'est vous qui me les avez donnés,"* and told her of finding them on her picture. She had forgotten them completely and was happy and grateful at having them returned to her at a moment in which she herself felt such need of them.

I went straight to the theatre from the Hotel Majestic, and that evening I acted with no sense of personal success at stake. I began to realize from that moment that in playing, as in any other art, one should abolish the personal and try to place one's instrument at the service of a higher, disembodied force ; the more perfect the instrument, the finer the force that would choose to make use of it. I suddenly realized the years of work ahead, the necessity of working with an ever-increasing intensity, and particularly the necessity of a wide range of experience embracing to the greatest possible degree the finest dramatic material. For the first time the thought tangibly crossed my mind : where are the repertory theatres in this country ? The answer came to me in a flash of surprised realization : "There are none." The question "Why ?" followed inevitably, and from then on the problem of supplying this lack in the scope of the American Theatre became my incessant and persistent obsession.

The opening night of "The Swan" took place in an absolute downpour of drenching rain. It was considered a bad omen by many of the older actors in the cast, especially for a light comedy. Young Mr. Baker, who had so splendidly adapted the play into English, sent us an amusing telegram : "Remember what is good weather for ducks is good weather for 'Swans.' " He was a true prophet ; the play was an overwhelming success.

The next morning Mme. Duse telephoned me ; she had read all the notices, which were magnificent, but she wanted to know if I myself felt happy. I could scarcely answer her question. I felt almost as if I had not been there at all. I was too busy struggling into "another square" ; a square into which she was mainly responsible for pushing me. I did not yet feel at home or lucid in it.

I saw Mme. Duse many times in the weeks that followed, either on the stage or personally. I sat in my first row seat at the initial matinée of "Donna del Mare" (Ibsen's "Lady from the Sea") at the Century Theatre. There followed "Cosi Sia," "Porta Chiusa," "Ghosts," and "Città Morta." Each play was given two performances, and through close study I began to realize even more poignantly the amazing perfection of her technique — a technique that concealed technique.

Arthur Symons is probably the only writer who has succeeded in describing the quality, difference, and perfection of Duse's acting. In his book "Studies in the Seven Arts" he says of her :

"The reason why Duse is the greatest actress in the world is that she has a more subtle nature than any other actress, and that she expresses her nature more simply.

All her acting seems to come from a great depth, and to be only half telling profound secrets. No play has ever been profound enough, and simple enough, for this woman to say everything she has to say in it. When she has thrilled one, or made one weep, or exalted one with beauty, she seems to be always holding back something else. Her supreme distinction comes from the kind of melancholy wisdom which remains in her face after the passions have swept over it. Other actresses seem to have heaped up into one great fictitious moment all the scattered energies of their lives, the passions that have come to nothing, the sensations that have withered before they flowered, the thoughts that have never quite been born. The stage is their life ; they live only for those three hours of the night ; before and after are the intervals between the acts. But to Duse those three hours are the interval in an intense, consistent, strictly personal life ; and, the interval over, she returns to herself, as after an interruption.

"And this unique fact makes for her the particular quality of her genius. When she is on the stage she does not appeal to us with the conscious rhetoric of the actress ; she lets us overlook her, with an unconsciousness which study has formed into a second nature.

"To act as Duse acts, with an art which is properly the antithesis of what we call acting, is, no doubt, to fail in a lesser thing in order to triumph in a greater. Her greatest moments are the moments of most intense quietness ; she does not send a shudder through the whole

house, as Sarah Bernhardt does, playing on one's nerves
as on a violin. 'Action,' with her as with Rimbaud, 'is
a way of spoiling something,' when once action has mastered thought, and got loose to work its own way in the
world. It is a disturbance, not an end in itself ; and
the very expression of emotion, with her, is all a restraint, the quieting down of a tumult until only the
pained reflection of it glimmers out of her eyes, and
trembles among the hollows of her cheeks. Contrast her
art with the art of Irving, to whom acting is at once a
science and a tradition. To Irving acting is all that the
word literally means ; it is an art of sharp, detached, yet
always delicate movement ; he crosses the stage with intention, as he intentionally adopts a fine, crabbed, personal, highly conventional elocution of his own ; he is an
actor, and he acts, keeping nature, or the too close semblance of nature, carefully out of his composition. He
has not gone to himself to invent an art wholly personal,
wholly new ; his acting is no interruption of an intense
inner life, but a craftsmanship into which he has put all
he has to give. It is an art wholly rhetoric, that is to say
wholly external ; his emotion moves to slow music, crys-
tallizes into an attitude, dies upon a long-drawn-out
word. And it is this external, rhetorical art, this dram-
atized oratory, that we have always understood as acting,
until Duse came upon the stage with new ideas and a new
method. At once rhetoric disappeared, with all that is
obvious in its loss, as well as what is somewhat less obviously gained by it. Duse's art, in this, is like the art

of Verlaine in French poetry ; always suggestion, never statement, always a renunciation. It comes into the movement of all the arts, as they seek to escape from the bondage of form, by a new, finer mastery of form, wrought outwards from within, not from without inwards. And it conquers almost the last obstacle, as it turns the one wholly external art, based upon mere imitation, existing upon the commonest terms of illusion, triumphing by exaggeration, into an art wholly subtle, almost spiritual, a suggestion, an evasion, a secrecy."

AGAIN I felt the stultifying effect of a "successful" engagement and once more started on the war-path for more work. This time I set my heart on a production for special matinées, of Hauptmann's "Hannele's Himmelfahrt." I had no money, so I applied to Mrs. C. C. Rumsey, always an enthusiastic backer of artists, for financial aid. It happened that just at this time she was contemplating some theatrical ventures in collaboration with John D. Williams, a man with a definite genius for dramatic production. He became interested in the idea of directing "Hannele," and Mrs. Rumsey supplied the necessary money for these performances. I was to engage the company (somewhat recruited from the cast of "The Swan"), secure the Cort Theatre for the selected afternoons, and look after the announcements and publicity. All of these things I did according to Mr. Williams's instructions. I also procured the aid of George Copeland for the musical end of the production. He chose the music and himself conducted the orchestra with his usual unerring taste. To my great joy he selected for the funeral march Debussy's "Nuages," which exactly interpreted the kind of victorious glamour which, to the child Hannele, was synonymous with death.

I called the first rehearsal as planned with Mr. Williams. A few moments before the work was to begin, I received a message from him saying he could not be there until the following day, but to go ahead with the reading of the play. This we did, and at the next rehearsal I again received a letter from him saying he could not be present for several days and instructing me to start "breaking in" the production. I had no experience whatever as a director. But having called the company, knowing time was short and bearing his orders in mind I started as best I could. I had a very definite conception of the play and the work progressed fairly well. Mr. Williams was unfortunately ill during the entire rehearsal period, and the whole responsibility fell upon my shoulders. I think I could never have reached production if it had not been for the loyalty and constructive help given me by the stage hands of the Cort Theatre. I was totally ignorant of lighting and all the other technicalities of stage presentations. The "heads of departments" — carpenter, electrician, and property man — for some reason took pity on me and efficiently and magnanimously "covered" me on the entire physical production of this difficult play. I can never express in words my gratitude for their whole-hearted co-operation.

Towards the last of the rehearsals, when the united problems of a dramatic presentation such as "Hannele" bore down on me with an almost overwhelming force, I sent an S. O. S. to Mme. Duse, then playing in New Orleans, and immediately received the following telegram :

"Ayez tous les souhaits. Ne doutez jamais de vous-même. Vous trouverez une nouvelle force dans le nouvel effort. Tout sera bien. Bon salut.

Eleonora Duse"

Up until the final dress rehearsal I received assurances of Mr. Williams's ultimate appearance, and because of this, the posters and program carried the agreed-upon announcement : Play under the direction of John D. Williams.   He was unable to turn up at all, and the play had to go on with what faulty direction I had been able to give it.   My duties as producer had been so strenuous that I had barely had three rehearsals on my own part of "Hannele."   At the opening matinée I was so tired and so frightened that I broke down and cried in Basil Rathbone's arms on my first entrance.   He played the Schoolmaster "Christ" part, and very beautifully.

The next day our notices were divided fifty-fifty. Some critics raved in appreciation, others raved in angry denunciation.   On the whole I was happy, for in both praise and blame there was a spirit so definite that it bore the marks of importance ; at least we were not "damned with faint praise" : to me the ultimate verdict of real failure.

One innovation called forth various opposite opinions, and was even thought worthy of a flattering editorial in *The Sun* : I had announced that, in view of the delicate quality of the play, no one would be seated after the rise of the curtain — in fact, that the doors would be locked and the late comers would have either to leave (which some did in great anger) or wait till the end of the scene. I held the curtain fifteen minutes after the hour announced in the paper and then rang up. Among the people caught in the lobby was Mr. Alexander Woollcott, who behaved charmingly about it and agreed on the rightness of the policy. In his review the next day he stressed the advisability of managers' getting together in a real effort to stamp out the nuisance of late arrivals, pointing out the annoyance both to public and to players of such carelessness. The custom of barring out late comers during the opening number is taken for granted at concerts, and he felt that it could be established in theatres if managers would consistently collaborate in such a scheme.

"Hannele" was unexpectedly successful, and the two matinées scheduled were extended to four. Through my experience with this play my interest in direction was definitely awakened ; the scope offered by the interpretation and fusion into a rhythmical whole of the elements involved in dramatic presentation became tempting and fascinating to me. I started to work for a knowledge of the technical end of the stage itself : scenery, lighting, and such problems. My friends the stage hands at the

Cort were sympathetic and patient with me, and I learned much from them.

Soon after the final matinée of "Hannele," Mme. Simone sent me word that she would like me to play with her for some special performances in French of Bataille's play, "La Vierge Folle." As usual thirsting for work, I went to secure Mr. Miller's permission.

Dear Gilbert Miller! No manager was ever kinder or more considerate, but he was getting a little tired of my restlessness and complained that other actresses in successful plays were satisfied and were not everlastingly annoying their managements with incessant demands for extra activity! This time he at first point-blank refused permission. Simone went to him, I went to him again, and finally he gave in, but not without trying many tactics which he hoped would discourage me; the cleverest of these was a warning that Simone was a *really* great actress and would "make me look like ten cents." I told him that the greater she was the better, so far as I was concerned; I felt there would be much to learn from working with her, and that was all that mattered to me.

Playing in a foreign language was a curious sensation. It was difficult to keep one's inner train of thought from slipping into English, but very soon I became accustomed to it and found French, as a language, a wonderful medium for acting. The method of acting in France differs greatly from the usual Anglo-Saxon manner. The tempo is faster, more staccato; there are very few pauses; the gestures are more vivid, more exaggerated

— in fact, the whole effect is more flamboyantly dramatic. This experience was very interesting to me ; in
sheer self-defence I was forced to accentuate and project
my points with twice the intensity I would normally have
used ; had I not done so I would have seemed totally
lacking in vitality and color.

Mme. Duse was expected to return to New York in a
few days ; I received a wire from her during my work
in the French play :

*"Très heureuse vous retrouver en pleine bataille. Tout
sera bien. Tous souhaits. Tendrement.*

Duse"

Then suddenly the news of her death in Pittsburgh
came as a terrible shock to the many who loved and admired her. That such a vital, ardent force had left our
world seemed inconceivably hard to bear, or even to believe.

To anyone who had been privileged to know her, it
was her gallant, unconquerable spirit, her courage, her
childlike, infectious gaiety, as well as her great wisdom
and compassion, that one remembered best. The legend that has somehow grown up around her, stressing
only sadness and brooding melancholy, making of her a
sort of long-suffering, martyred saint, betrays utterly the
many-faceted richness, the ever-young enthusiasm of her
dynamic personality. She looked always toward the Future ; she had an unfailing belief in Youth ; she loved all
truly living things. She stood "free and high up" both
in her life and in her work.

X

THE long run of "The Swan" was cut short in June by the Actors' Equity strike.

I decided that instead of spending a holiday in Europe, I would go to Jasper Deeter's theatre in Rose Valley and have a try at "The Master Builder." I had heard of Deeter's experiment from Ann Harding, who had worked a great deal under his direction. The thing that interested me most in the Rose Valley Theatre was the uncompromising choice of plays : Deeter refused to work on any material that did not in some way conform to his high standard of what a play should be. He was also an ardent believer in the repertory system, which more and more filled my thoughts. The summer before, Ann Harding had played Hilda Wangel at his theatre, and I suggested that I should at first play Mrs. Solness with her in "The Master Builder" and then try myself in the part of Hilda.

Deeter and I did not entirely agree on the interpretation of the play, and arranged that I should direct the play myself for the performances in which I was to play the leading rôle. I took a house near the theatre and started work. I found a boy called Sydney Machat, who, though far too young for the part of the Master Builder, had power and understanding enough to give an amazingly interesting interpretation of this difficult rôle. It was fascinating stuff to work on. I suppose it is one of the most intriguing, stimulating and elusive plays that have ever been written. We threw ourselves into it with all the intensity and vitality with which we were bubbling over. The performances were not particularly good, but they were immensely useful to me as a kind of preliminary sketch, for I was as determined as ever to play Hilda Wangel in New York some day, and as the thought of a repertory theatre following along the lines of the European state theatres grew clearer in my mind, I felt that "The Master Builder" should be one of the first plays on the schedule.

"The Swan" re-opened for a short New York engagement at the Empire Theatre in the early fall. I was thrilled to find myself playing in this old house again, and overwhelmed by the thought of dressing in the room that had belonged to so many great artists. My continued success had of course made life easier for me. I had plenty of money, had even bought a car, and also a dog, for it was during my New York engagement at the Cort that my Cairn terrier "Tosca" came into my life. She is still with me, thank goodness and has been a loyal and wonderful friend to me all these years. A sturdy, stalwart little dog she is too ! We are both a little older and a little wiser now, but our devotion to each other has undergone no change. She never misses a performance, and has traveled with me wherever I have been.

Mother joined me in Chicago, where "The Swan" played for ten weeks. I had a charming apartment on the Lake shore, and Mother and I enjoyed a life of luxury, remembering with laughter and tears the hardships we had been through together. It was fun to be able to order anything you wanted to eat and to have it served in state in a comfortable sitting-room! It was fun to have a car! It was fun not to have to count every nickel before spending it! Yes, it was fun to be a successful young star; life was good indeed. Sometimes I would be afraid of getting spoiled, afraid of growing "soft." Now and then, as a test, I would deliberately discipline myself, just to make sure I wasn't losing my point of view; would limit myself to twenty cents for dinner and take it in a lunch-room; or take a streetcar or a subway instead of a taxi; I tried to keep guard against the insidious joys of prosperity.

And then suddenly and ever more and more recurrent, the thought would come: What now? Is this all? What next?

I suppose I was not really cut out for a life of ease. In any case I have certainly succeeded in inventing difficulties for myself! That final season in "The Swan" was the last I've had of that kind of comfortable, unworried existence. From that time on I really swung into action. There followed an experience which was harder

than anything I had imagined. I am glad to have had
it ; for, ever since, I have felt that nothing could compare with it for sheer stress and worry.

Mercedes de Acosta had written two plays, "Jehanne
d'Arc" and "The Mother of Christ." Both plays were
interesting as to subject and were treated with a simple
poetry that gave promise of fine performance. Norman
Bel-Geddes became most enthusiastic over them, and the
three of us decided to bring about their production.
Geddes designed two of his amazing "stages" on which
they were to be played, and together we worked out the
technical difficulties involved. Then the mad idea came
to us : why not produce "Jehanne d'Arc" first in Paris ?
I could play in French as easily as in English, and it
would be the first American production seen in France :
written by an American and directed and played by
Americans. Firmin Gémier happened to be in New
York at the time we were at the height of our plans and
gave us every encouragement, waxing eloquent over the
beauties of the play and Geddes's production-ideas, not
to speak of my French. He promised to secure us a
theatre in Paris and guide us through any difficulties that
might present themselves, though of course there would
be few ! He felt certain the total cost of the venture
would not exceed $7,000.

To be on the safe side we raised $12,000. People who
invested capital in the scheme would be repaid by the
profits earned by the play when presented in New York,

for we would of course return from Paris in triumph,
and in America the play would certainly be a huge success, particularly backed by its Paris "sensation" ! Three
more ludicrous, three more pathetically sincere and
trusting children, never set off on a wild adventure !
On receiving a cable from Gémier : "Sail with confidence
on the *Mauretania*," we embarked with high hopes,
laughing scornfully at anyone who dared to show scepti-
cism of our plan.

The first blow came when Gémier informed us that
we had as yet no theatre. We had understood him to
say that he would have everything planned for us. Instead, his only suggestion was that we play at his theatre,
the Odéon. After examining the stage, Geddes found
that would be out of the question ; there was not nearly
enough room for the colossal structure of parallels and
platforms he had devised as scenery. Also, the Odéon
being a repertory theatre, we could play only three or
four times a week, and it would take three or four hours
to set up the aforementioned parallels or take them down
again. It would only be practicable to use a theatre
with a big stage on which they could be left permanently
standing during the run of the production.

It became increasingly and alarmingly obvious that
Mr. Gémier was less enthusiastic at home than he had
been abroad ! After several conferences on our next
step, the three of us were in complete accord on at least
one point : we were determined not to give in ! Come

what may, we had said we were going to produce the
play there, and produce it we would.   We would prove
that Americans are not so easily beaten !

Then came our search for a theatre.   We found there
were only four stages in Paris that could accommodate
Geddes's setting.   They all seemed unprocurable.   At
last, through Gabriel Astruc, to whom we had been
referred, we secured the Porte St. Martin.   The terms
seemed a bit staggering, taking into consideration the
production cost suggested in New York by Gémier, and
I began to feel really worried about money.   For the
four walls of the theatre, for thirty days' use, we had to
pay in cash $7,000.   There remained the cost of the
production, the costumes, the employees of the theatre,
the rehearsal costs for actors, supers, and stage hands, and
the publicity and advertising.   I saw well enough that
our $12,000 would be woefully insufficient, but we were
in with all six feet and there was nothing to do but
carry on.

In the agreement with the Porte St. Martin was the
stipulation that we must use the permanent company of
actors employed by that theatre.   Then came the question of supers.   Geddes at first insisted he could not do
with fewer than two hundred and fifty ; this we finally
persuaded him to reduce to one hundred and fifty.   The
head of the supers' union insisted we must use all French
people, but Geddes had visions of very tall men for
Jehanne's knights and found the Frenchmen too small
— he wanted Russians.   A compromise with the union

was reached, and we were allowed to engage fifty Russian exiles, as against one hundred Frenchmen. These Russians were an amazing lot, from all walks of life : princes, soldiers, officers, schoolteachers, young university men. Most of them spoke German, and a few a little French, but not all of them, and this complicated the already appalling language-problem, for Geddes couldn't speak a word of anything but English, or rather American ! He had to have two interpreters, one for French and one for Russian. He had brought with him from his New York office two assistants ; one spoke a little French, the other not a word. Never shall I forget the chaos of these rehearsals ; they were bedlam !

The first reading and rehearsals of the play were to take place in the Trocadéro. Our production was to be presented under the patronage of the Ministers des Beaux Arts, and we were informed that the big hall at the Trocadéro would be at our disposal gratis for preliminary rehearsals. This seemed like a friendly gesture, and we felt very grateful. The enormous company was called at nine-thirty in the morning. Norman's assistants brought in the model of the scenery, and I was to read the play and at the same time explain to the actors how the setting worked.

They had never seen anything like it before and were really impressed and on the whole enthusiastic about the whole idea of the play. We did nothing that day but sit in the big hall for three or four hours doing this preparatory work.

The next day I called a rehearsal for nine A. M. in the same place. I arrived there a few minutes before the hour and to my amazement was told by the stage manager of the Trocadéro that my company could not work there any more, on account of the "destruction" we had caused the day before. I was then presented with a bill for several thousand francs ! This I refused to pay at the time, laughingly asserting that I saw no reason that *we* should pay for repairs on the Trocadéro, repairs that had obviously been neglected for many years.

Our money was getting appallingly low, and the great crusade for funds started. This brought me into many amazing situations. We went to see the American Ambassador, the kindly and charming Mr. Herrick. We explained our growing plight. Of course he could do nothing officially, but he gave us letters to various wealthy people, or indications of where they could be found.

I remember attacking Ogden Armour in his lair at the Ritz Hotel. I found him alone in his sitting-room, shivering before the fire. He looked up in amazement at seeing a strange young female ; I remember he had on orange-brown shoes with bumps at the toes.

I told him I was very sorry to disturb him but he must let me have $3,000 immediately. I think he was intrigued and startled by the violence of my attack. When he found out the reason for my demand he informed me that only once in his life had he given money to the theatre and that he had regretted it ever since. I told him that "the honor of America was at stake," that he must help us carry on our purpose. I begged him, cajoled him, and finally wore him out ; for, picking up his hat and growling at me to follow him, he walked out of the Ritz, across the Place Vendôme to his bank, and growling at me again to "sit down and wait" disappeared into an inner office. In a few moments he returned and flinging a bundle in my lap said, "I don't know why I'm doing this ; never did such a thing in my life and don't want to do it now, but there you are !" I shook hands with him gratefully and said, "If ever you're broke and I have a dollar I'll give you fifty cents !" At this he burst into laughter and we parted the best of friends.

Rehearsals went on ; we were now working on the stage of the Porte St. Martin. Dress rehearsals began under inconceivable difficulties. Geddes had had an entire electrical equipment of the most advanced type shipped from New York. No one in Paris knew how to work it ; everything was considered "impossible" because our methods of stagecraft were so unfamiliar to the French stage hands and electricians. They looked upon us as three lunatics. Geddes was horribly handicapped by not knowing the language. The dress rehearsals were a torture. Mercedes and I sold everything we possessed and still the bills came in, and everything had to be paid in cash. Even the actors and supers had to be paid ten days in advance. The night of the dress rehearsal things went wrong with some of the clothes, and Geddes in his excitement gave the wardrobe-lady a rap on the arm with his megaphone.   Then there was pandemonium, in the midst of which Geddes escaped !

The company was like a hornet's nest.   We were all *"des sauvages," "des barbares Américains."*   The actors refused to open until he had apologized.   I rushed all over Paris looking for him, but he was worn out and had hidden away somewhere in despair.

The next day I called the company together and begged them with tears to play that night.   They finally consented to go through with it for my sake.   I think they really felt sorry for me.   The opening performance that evening was a nightmare.   I was so nervous and exhausted I simply couldn't play.   I had no inner peace and had been robbed of the last vestige of self-confidence, faith, or hope.   I remember that the scenery made a great impression ; some parts of the play, mostly the pageantry, were enthusiastically applauded.

One funny incident stands out in my mind.   In the battle scene my knights and I were surrounded by the enemy and gradually forced backwards up the parallels, till finally, at a height of fifteen or twenty feet above the stage-level, I was to stand alone, all my soldiers having been killed, raising my banner high, until I was dragged down by the attacking army.   One of my knights, a huge Russian boy, became so interested in the fight that he simply would not give in, and being almost a giant he found it quite easy to dislodge the approaching foe and prevent them from capturing me.   He could not under-

stand a word of French or English and finally summoning
up my slight knowledge of Russian I yelled at him
through the din : "Please die, won't you ! I implore
you to die !" He looked at me in amazement and then,
roaring with laughter, lay down and "died" — to the
great relief of the "enemy," who wanted to get on with
the scene !

At last it was over and I was about to drag my weary
self to my dressing-room when the two stage managers
seized hold of me in great excitement, shouting something about my having to make "the announcement."

It seems it is the custom in France for the leading actor
after a première to step before the curtain and make a
formal announcement giving the name of the play and
the name of the author. I had not the faintest idea of
what to say, but it is a definite formula and I repeated
it after the stage manager, parrot-fashion : *"La pièce que
nous avons eu l'honneur de présenter premièrement
devant vous est 'Jehanne d'Arc' par Mercédès de Acosta."*

The next day the notices were all bad. The play was
attacked, I was attacked, Norman Geddes was the only
one who was not completely annihilated in the press.
The production itself had made quite an impression ;
they did not particularly like it, but it was new and im-
posing. A few people of the *"avant-garde"* were enthusiastic about the entire presentation and still talk
about it today with great admiration and a feeling of re-
gret that, as they say, Paris was not ready for such modern
stagecraft at that time. They all feel that, were it to be

repeated now, it would be received with great appreciation.

As far as I am concerned I am willing to allow that
assertion to remain unproven !

XI

BACK in New York I found it immediately necessary to start playing. We all returned penniless and discouraged instead of rich and triumphant, but it was all in the mad game called "the Theatre" and there was nothing to do but begin work on something else at once.

None of the plays that were submitted to me appealed to me, and the plays I wanted to do didn't appeal to the managers. The outlook was not very hopeful. Suddenly Dudley Digges, who was directing for the Actors' Theatre, sent me a play by Schnitzler, "The Call of Life." It was a fine, interesting play and I gladly agreed to start work in it. In the company I found an old friend, Egon Brecher, who had played the Sparrow in "Liliom," following Dudley Digges ; Alice John, another old friend from "The Swan" and "Hannele" was also in the cast, which was a fine one, including Katherine Alexander, Thomas Chalmers, Douglas Dumbrille, and others.

It was pleasant working with Digges, and the whole period of rehearsals seemed peaceful and restful after my recent struggles. The play unfortunately was not successful, and I tried to persuade the Actors' Theatre to stage "The Master Builder" for their next production ; but they were afraid that it would prove unpopular and would not undertake it at that time. I then decided to go into management for myself and produce it for some special matinées, as a start. Brecher agreed to play Solness with me, and Alice John, Mrs. Solness. We rehearsed for only two weeks and gave our first matinée at the Maxine Elliott Theatre in early October. Through Noel Coward I met the young scenic designer G. E. Calthrop ; she had come with him to New York to stage his play "The Vortex," which had opened with such brilliant success a few weeks before. She agreed to arrange the scenery, and out of some old stuff that we borrowed from Charles Dillingham, which she repainted and refurnished, managed to set the play quite respectably.

To my amazement we had a great success. The critics were kind and the public enthusiastic. The four matinées announced were extended to twelve, and then I took the Princess Theatre and we started a regular run.

With the thought of repertory ever in my mind, Brecher and I decided to start rehearsals of "John Gabriel Borkman," and while still playing "The Master Builder" at the Princess, we presented "Borkman" for special matinées at the Booth, since the stage of the Princess was too small for this more important production. Mrs. Calthrop again designed the scenery, this time on a more lavish scale.

The dress rehearsal of "Borkman" stands out in my

mind as a mixture of tragedy and farce. Most dress rehearsals are apt to be gloomy affairs at best, but this one ended on a note of irresistible comedy, in definite contrast to the stark content of the drama. We were all very tired. Brecher and I had played a performance of "The Master Builder" that evening, and the dress rehearsal was to take place at the Booth, after midnight. It was of course nearer two A.M. when the first act was set and everyone ready in costume to begin. One mishap followed the other ; the scenery had never been set up before and, as it was fairly difficult stuff, the night dragged on endlessly until about six-thirty A.M. we started on the last act. By this time we were exhausted to the point of hysteria, and the thought of playing the first performance on that very same afternoon filled us with horror. The last-act set is a double one : the first scene is in front of Borkman's house, and during a black-out the house disappears, some gauzes are flown, and when the lights slowly come on again, John Gabriel and Ella are discovered toiling up an "icy pathy" against snow peaks, and play the last few moments of the action on a small bench set several feet above stage-level ; the snow begins to fall just before the final curtain. During the black-out Brecher and I crept gropingly across the stage to the side, searching for the steps in the icy path, with which we were totally unfamiliar, and became enveloped in the voluminous folds of the black-velvet side curtain, from which we with difficulty extricated ourselves, battling our way out during the first lines of our dialogue. "Where are we going, John Gabriel? Why must we climb so high?" We finally emerged rather the worse for the tussle with the curtain, which had seemed strangely and fiendishly alive, and struggled up the icy path to our bench. We still kept in our stern and tragic characters, however, and proceeded with the solemn, noble dialogue.

Brecher was tremendously impressive in this final scene. His make-up was exceptionally fine. He wore a beard and moustache of iron-gray, and his eyes looked hollow and feverish. All was well, until the snow began to fall! The snow-bag had been filled by the property man too hastily, and now with devastating effect its contents descended upon us, as we desperately tried to carry on as though nothing were wrong, amidst a positive deluge of huge paper snowflakes. They went up our noses and into our mouths and settled in fantastic patterns on Brecher's head. At one moment we had to look straight into each other's eyes; I had been dreading this moment, for I felt hysteria descending upon me, but here the moment was: we looked at each other, standing there hung like Christmas trees with the paper snowflakes, and suddenly, amidst a final flurry of tremendous violence, a coat-hanger descended from the snow-bag and fastened itself in Brecher's beard! We burst into roars and screams of uncontrollable laughter. It was too much, we could be solemn no longer! Brecher threw himself on the ground and laughed as only he can laugh. He rolled down the slope onto the stage-level while I collapsed on the seat in an absolute paroxysm of mirth. With tears of laughter pouring down our faces we decided there was no use in going on then ; there was nothing to do but go home and rest, praying for help at the performance.   It was by now eight A.M. and the curtain rose on the matinée at two-thirty.

We looked for nothing but disaster that afternoon, but the gods took pity on us, and the performance was received with "bravos" and endless applause from public and press.   It seemed incredible !   The play had gone as smoothly as though we had had three dress rehearsals, and to Brecher's and my infinite gratitude there was *no snow !*

Along with my belief in the repertory system, the idea that popular prices should prevail began to develop in my mind.   I decided to see what would happen and gave two special performances at ten-thirty A.M. at the Booth Theatre to $1.50 top-price, one of "The Master Builder" and one of "Borkman."   Both times the house was entirely sold out.   This was all very encouraging and began to prove to me that my dream of establishing a repertory theatre, presenting great plays at popular prices, was not so impossible as most people would have me believe.

But I needed a little time to make thorough and complete preparations, and I decided to take the two Ibsen plays on tour for the balance of the season, meanwhile working out my plan in detail.   Two points became very clear to me :

1. There definitely existed in New York an audience for the type of plays I wished to produce.

2. This audience was largely made up of people with modest means : probably comprising the same elements that so noticeably supported music, in the cheaper seats (the inevitable home of most real music-lovers) : students, workers, thinking people to whom art and literature in any form were real necessities and not *only* for amusement.

My plan suddenly crystallized and in a couple of hours I wrote out a schedule covering the first ten weeks of work. I found this slip of paper the other day and was amused to see that with scarcely a change it had been put into execution when the Civic Repertory Theatre opened.

We were to start with a repertory of four plays : I counted on the two Ibsen plays already running, and to these I decided to add Tchekov's "The Three Sisters" and Benavente's "Saturday Night." Then every four or five weeks after the opening of the theatre, we would produce a new play, until at some future date, when our repertory should be large enough and flexible enough, we might on certain very difficult productions take a longer rehearsal period. For our fifth play I chose Goldoni's "La Locandiera," then "Twelfth Night" of Shakespeare, "Inheritors" by Glaspell, and an eighth play to be determined later. In this way by the end of our first season our repertory would include eight plays widely different in character and feeling. The top-price of $1.50 was adopted, with the cheapest seats at fifty cents.

One day in Cincinnati I called the company together and told them the whole scheme. They were enthusiastic and with one accord decided to follow me in an effort to carry it through. These actors became the nucleus of the Civic Repertory Theatre Company. They were : Egon Brecher, Beatrice Terry, J. Sayre Crawley, Harold Moulton, Sydney Machat, Ruth Wilton, and Beatrice de Neergaard. The next step was to discuss financial ways and means, the finding of a suitable theatre, the handling of the publicity. My business manager was then Charles Heede, but as I needed him with me on the tour, I wired Mary Duggett, who by this time was Mrs. Stuart Benson, to join me in Detroit, and having explained the entire situation asked her to work as my personal representative and get things started in New York.

I at first thought of Walter Hampden's theatre, since he had announced his intention of touring all the following season. It was a large theatre with plenty of stage-space, always vitally important to the repertory system, but the rental asked was very high and the management did not approve of the popular-price idea ; they felt it would lower the standard of their house. This proved, in fact, to be the case everywhere : no manager wanted to let his theatre to popular-price attractions. It seemed like an insuperable obstacle. But on this point I would

not give in, for it was the crux of my whole project.   My
great desire was to create a theatre for the service of the
People.   From the very beginning there was no commercial angle to my plan : the state repertory theatres of
Europe are all subsidized ; I could not see why America
should not have a repertory theatre subsidized by private
capital in the same way that its opera companies and sym-
phony orchestras are.   Why should the drama be the
only neglected art ?   Why should it alone be thought
an unnecessary factor in the cultural lives of the people,
when it has been proved time and again to be one of the
most vital ?   Millions were spent on libraries, museums,
and music, but the Theatre was an outcast.   I knew from
personal experience as a child what the popular-priced
repertories of Europe meant to the public.   I had myself missed them tremendously during my early years in
this country, had in fact been amazed at not finding so
much as *one*.

No ! the whole scheme might prove to be a mad one,
but there would be no compromise.   If it failed, it
would fail in its true colors.   On this point I was
adamant.

I felt it was important to raise sufficient money to
guarantee a twenty-week trial of the plan.   All the actors
were to receive a twenty-week guarantee in their contracts ; the thing must be given a sense of possible perma-
nence from the start.   A few weeks would not be a fair
test.

The theatre situation looked very bleak for us, when I

was told of an old theatre on Fourteenth Street, just west
of Sixth Avenue.   It was in bad shape, they said, but
could be cleaned up and renovated.   It had a huge stage
and a seating capacity of about 1100.   At the time, it
was being used for Italian plays, and previous to that had
been a burlesque house.   On my return to New York
at the end of May, when our Ibsen tour closed, I went
to Fourteenth Street to look it over.   I was immediately
struck by a sense of dignity that reminded me slightly of
my feelings when rehearsing at Daly's.   I felt sure that
in days gone by this theatre had held an important and
enviable position.   Inside it was indescribably dirty and
dilapidated ; but the proscenium arch rose in a beautiful curve, the lines of the house, balcony and gallery,
were harmonious and friendly, and the big stage, with its
tremendously high grid, was perfect for housing many
productions.   I felt immediately that this was where I
wanted to start work.   As I went through the pass door
onto the stage, I looked down suddenly and saw Madame
Duse's face gazing up at me from an old Italian newspaper.   I picked it up : perhaps it was a telegram after
all, saying *"Tout sera bien !"*

There were difficulties in securing the theatre ; the
Italians didn't want to give it up.   I left Mrs. Benson
and Heede in charge of negotiations and went to Europe
for a short holiday before starting on what I knew would
be a strenuous job.

On my return six weeks later, I was told by the ship
reporters that the news had "broken" that very morning :

the Civic Repertory was to open at the Fourteenth Street Theatre, in October. I was jubilant at having secured the old house, on which I had set my heart, and as I drove past it on my way home from the ship I saw between laughter and tears that "the boys," the stage hands, had placed a large sign "Welcome Eva Le Gallienne" above the entrance doors !

ALTHOUGH Benavente's "Saturday Night" was an intensely difficult play, especially for such a young and inexperienced director as myself, it was the Tchekov play I was the most anxious about. "Saturday Night" was "theatre," not simple theatre, it's true, but depending enormously on physical production ; I had worked out all the technical end of the direction in the greatest detail, so as to have it all clearly established before actual rehearsals started. But "The Three Sisters" was so much more than mere theatre — it was almost the antithesis of it in a sense. To succeed in accurately projecting its myriad nuances and imperceptibly shifting moods, a very intimate and personal knowledge of the play must permeate everyone associated with it ; the actors must become imbued with its very essence. I felt it would be a great help to use a completely untheatrical method of work on "The Three Sisters," particularly as the company were not yet accustomed to playing together. I invited them to come and work in the country out at Westport. We took over a small inn on the Wilton road, and for nearly three weeks worked quietly and informally on the play.

The company consisted of all the people who had been on tour with the Ibsen plays, and, besides these, Paul Leyssac, Leona Roberts, Hardie Albright, Alan Campbell, Rose Hobart, and Alan Birmingham.

We sat around in the beautiful fields and woods near Weston trying to identify ourselves with the various characters ; we called each other by their names and frequently started work by discussing in character things not actually in the text. Then suddenly someone would give an actual cue and the discussion would be carried on in Tchekov's own words. This gave us a tremendous sense of ease and reality. It was not until we moved into town and started rehearsing on the stage that I began giving actual shape to the performance. We were all in love with the play, and I still feel it is the most beautiful of Tchekov's works, though most people consider "The Cherry Orchard" superior.

We rehearsed five weeks, working on all four plays that were to constitute our immediate repertory. It was hard work, but "frightfully thrilling" and I was very happy.

I received countless warnings from all sides. Repertory was an impossibility in New York ; the public would not take the trouble to look up the schedule. I replied that as repertory had never been tried, it was therefore an unknown quantity ; and the public certainly took the

trouble to look up opera schedules —why not theatre?
Another favorite line was : The prices are too low, the
public will take for granted that it's a cheap attraction ;
they would be just as willing to pay $2.50 as $1.50.

What no one could seem to understand was that I
was not trying to *compete* with the commercial theatre.
Methods that hold good for it did not necessarily hold
good for what I had in mind. The commercial theatre
is fine and has a great and important place in life ; I
simply felt there was room for another and quite different type of theatre. The one cannot possibly interfere
with the other. Many people had the impression that
I had gone highbrow and was looking down with
lofty contempt on Broadway. What nonsense! I love
Broadway! Broadway has been very kind to me. I
simply felt the need of making an effort to widen the
scope of the word "theatre" in America. The word
"music" does not mean *only* jazz any more than it means
only Beethoven ; the word "book" implies a range staggering in its immensity. I felt that the word "theatre"
had been narrowed down to meaning a "current success,"
as if all literature were narrowed down to the current
"best seller." What a lot we should miss if all the literature of the past were suddenly to be removed from our
libraries! Was there, then, not room for a theatre
which, while it occasionally might house a current success, would also give shelter and life to the great dramatic
literature of all times and all countries? No! Not
"highbrow," not "lofty," above all *not* "arty." I was

simply obsessed by an idea which seemed to me practical and useful, and wanted to put it to the test.

The Civic Repertory Theatre opened on October 26th, 1926, with Benavente's "Saturday Night." The performance was not a success. The audience was kind and patient, but except for a few moments, the play never sprang into life. Next morning the papers were amazingly good-natured, I thought, but I was well aware of the fact that our first play was a failure. If our venture had depended on that production alone, we would have been beaten in a week.

But the very next evening — Tuesday the 27th — came our first performance of "The Three Sisters," and on that evening we were all very happy. The play was received with a real ovation, and the next morning the reviews were magnificent. On one throw we had lost, but on the second we had certainly won. "The Master Builder" and "Borkman" followed in rapid succession through the week. The packed houses that attended "The Three Sisters" and "The Master Builder" carried the weaker houses drawn by "Saturday Night" and "Borkman."

We immediately started rehearsals of "La Locandiera." I remember an amusing incident that happened at that time, one day when I was sitting on the darkened stage eating a sandwich and precariously drinking coffee out of a paper container. The actors were out for lunch and I was talking over some details with the stage manager, when a very young man with a very pink face

stumbled up the steps onto the stage and asked for Miss
Le Gallienne. I asked what I could do for him. He
stuttered out a few phrases to the effect that he had an
appointment to interview me for his college paper and
that it was his first interview . . . he broke off in the
middle of a sentence and gazed in bewilderment at my
surroundings, at the sandwich, the paper container, and
finally at my somewhat grubby and untidy self. Thinking he was probably confused, it being his first interview,
I determined to help him out and asked what he would
specially like me to talk about. He then burst out:
"Look here, though! Weren't you a star?" I said I
supposed I was. "Look here, though! Weren't you a
Broadway star?" Yes, I supposed so. "Look here,
though! How did you come to this?!" In the face of
the bursts of laughter with which the stage manager and
I greeted this last remark, the young man evidently
thought he had wandered into an asylum of dangerous
lunatics, for he turned rapidly and falling down the steps
into the auditorium disappeared out of my life. Poor
darling! I felt so sorry for him. He had probably
voiced the opinion of many others and incidentally had
given me one of the best laughs of my life.

It would be tedious to follow step by step every production of the Civic Repertory Theatre. We had a
frantically busy, happy life. I literally lived in the theatre, for besides rehearsing daily and playing I had to
attend partly to the executive end of things.

The production of "The Cradle Song" was a definite

milestone that season ; we turned people away at every performance.   I was very much blamed by some for not commercializing this great success by moving it up to Broadway for a long run at regular prices ; but what a fool I should have been to throw away one of the best cards in my repertory pack !   I should have been an even greater fool to break faith with the public !   By keeping to our strict repertory rule, in which no play, no matter how great its success, can be played more than four times a week, "The Cradle Song," instead of exhausting itself in a possible six months' run and then disappearing into the limbo of past productions, ran into its sixth season when it took its place in the repertory on our re-opening.

Our final production that first season was Susan Glaspell's "Inheritors," all too little known.   If I were a Mussolini I should make a rule that all young American people be forced to read it — that is, if they could not see it played (for of course if I were a Mussolini there would be subsidized repertory theatres in all the great cities of our country !).   "Inheritors" is not perhaps a "good play," but it is a burning challenge to America, full of indignation against the results of a too rapid, too greedy prosperity, in which the material has become the ultimate goal in complete disregard of spiritual and ethical values.   "Why did so much get shut out ?   Prosperous, I suppose.   That seems to set things, set them in *fear.*"   The United States was founded upon visions of a greater and finer life ; then we became blinded by dollars and Big Business ; the machinery of success became our God, and success could have but a material meaning in our eyes. We shall have to retrace our steps with humility and courage, in search of the Vision from which we have strayed so far. Miss Glaspell, in words which reveal her clear and gallant spirit, does not spare America, but only because she loves America so much ; she can't bear to see it fall so lamentably short of the ideals it was founded upon. The play is a tonic, and I heartily recommend it as an antidote to incipient smugness !

During the rehearsals of this play a great tragedy took place in the little world of our theatre. The young man who first played Solness with me in Rose Valley, Sydney Machat, had been a member of the company ever since I went into management with the Ibsen plays. He was a young actor of immense promise, an ardent worker, ever searching, never satisfied, always striving towards truth and perfection in his art. He had a brilliant mind ; for a boy of his age almost a startling mind. We all loved him and looked upon him with particular respect, for we were all convinced of his talent and felt he was already a great actor. He was nineteen at this time, a tall, raw-boned boy, with intense, boldly drawn features, who seemed consumed by an inner fire. He was restless, moody, violent. His long silences would suddenly be broken by hours of tempestuous talk. He had great humor, verging sometimes on the grotesque ; there was nothing gentle in it — it savored somewhat of Daumier, whose drawings, incidentally, he loved and studied closely.

On Saturday we were playing "Saturday Night" at the matinée, and the evening bill was "The Three Sisters," in which he played Solony. We had all noticed that he seemed strange and violent during the matinée ; but, knowing him, we thought he was in one of his Troll-moods and that by evening it would pass. His performance of Solony that night was especially interesting ; we all felt it. I was sitting in the wings waiting for my cue in the last act, and suddenly heard his voice saying his last lines :

"And restless seeks the stormy ocean,
As though in tempest, there were peace."

He spoke them quietly, but his voice had a strange un-earthly quality about it, and I remember thinking what a marvelous effect it gave the scene. It sounded like a great cord breaking ; the air seemed to vibrate in the silence that followed his exit.

After the performance the two young men who shared a dressing-room with Machat came to my room and told me they felt worried about Sydney ; he seemed so odd, they couldn't get him to leave the theatre, and he was talking in a sort of frenzy and wouldn't stop.

I begged them to take him home and not to leave him. I did not dare go to him myself, for he had seemed an-noyed with me all day and I feared my presence would irritate him further. But the two boys promised to stay with him and let me know if anything went wrong.

I went home and straight to bed, for I felt tired after two performances ; but I was troubled and could not seem to sleep. At five in the morning my bell rang and one of the young actors came in with a strange man, who was introduced to me as a well-known alienist. He told me Machat was temporarily insane and advised sending him to a hospital at once. It was dementia præcox. His overbrilliant mind had snapped under the strain of too feverish exertion. The doctor said that the life of the theatre was too much for him, that he should live very quietly, preferably in the country.

The horror of poor Sydney's illness cast a gloom over the company, but the weeks went by rapidly, taken up with the usual work at the theatre. We heard that he had joined his parents in Washington and was completely cured.

One day about three months later he appeared at the theatre with a friend of his. He seemed like a new being ; he had gained weight and looked healthy and clear-eyed. He announced his intention of rejoining the company and starting work at once.

Keeping the doctor's words in mind, I told him that this would be impossible : I had had to replace him, and there was no opening for him in our theatre. Every day he came back, begging for an opportunity to work. He couldn't live in the country ; his whole life was in the theatre ; he would go mad again without it ; in any case if he didn't work with us he would get a job somewhere else as an actor ; he could not, would not give it up. His friend joined in his supplication and I finally consented to his returning to the company. For over a month he worked with us, taking up his old parts and rehearsing an important rôle in "Inheritors," which was nearing production. No one could have seemed happier or saner than he. We all rejoiced at his complete recovery and it was good to have him there again. One evening after a particularly fine rehearsal I complimented him on his work in "Inheritors" and he seemed calm and content.

The next day work started at eleven A.M., but Machat was not called before two in the afternoon — he was not in the third act on which we worked all morning. A little after two I called his scene, and the stage manager told me he was not yet in the theatre. I was surprised, for the boy was such an enthusiastic worker and had never been known to be even a minute late. When two-thirty came I told the assistant stage manager to call up Machat's lodging house : possibly he had misunderstood the hour. When the assistant came back, he reported that someone had answered the telephone in a rather strange way, saying that Mr. Machat was ill, and had hung up very abruptly. The stage manager decided he had better go round to Sydney's lodgings and see for himself if anything was wrong. I shall never forget his face when he returned.   He came straight over to me, white as a sheet. "Machat has killed himself," he said and slumped into a chair.

All afternoon we hung about the stage in miserable little groups.   It was as though a heavy mist enveloped us all.   But the inexorable discipline of the theatre demanded action : the play must go on.   The performance that night was a difficult business.   There was a hush backstage ; we went through our parts as best we could, but our thoughts and hearts were with our lost comrade who had rebelled against life and broken with it.

To me the thought of him brings with it the memory of those lines he spoke so beautifully :

"And restless seeks the stormy ocean,
    As though in tempest there were peace. . ."

XII

At the close of the season, I went for a short trip to Europe. Aside from seeing Mother, I hoped to find a couple of interesting plays and perhaps see some good work in the theatres over there. I had seen absolutely nothing since the opening of the Civic Repertory; I was a complete prisoner at Fourteenth Street. The first year had been enormously encouraging. We had ended with a short tour which had been highly successful. Everything looked hopeful for the future.

The most interesting event of the summer in Paris was Isadora Duncan's recital, her first for many years outside of Russia. I had met Isadora several years before, and had seen her dance once at the Metropolitan Opera House, when I first came to America. She was deep in preparation for her coming recital when we reached Paris and lamented the fact that owing to lack of backing she would be unable to include many of the new things she had worked out, notably some Scriabine, since they required a larger orchestra and a choir of voices, and her backers refused to supply these. How monstrous it seemed that an artist of her importance should be hampered in such ways! She may have been impractical in her personal life, but her creed of work was clear and strong, and as with most great geniuses her vision was beyond a doubt practical. Her great artistic conceptions could have been realized had someone had the courage and faith to help her execute them.

The Mogador Theatre, on the afternoon of what proved to be her last recital, was packed. The excitement and emotion in the house were indescribable. I doubt if she ever had danced so marvelously as she did that day. She seemed to me to give to the dance the quality Duse gave to acting : a sort of cosmic understanding of all life, transmuted into sheer Beauty.

What a poor age we live in now ! The other day a young girl of twenty said to me : "I was born ten years too late ; I've missed everything ! I have never seen Bernhardt, Guitry, Pavlowa, Nijinsky and the Diaghileff Ballet, Yvette Guilbert, Réjane, Irving, Isadora Duncan, Duse. I've missed them all !" I thought to myself : "I wouldn't change places with you for anything ; not even to be twenty again !"

In Paris I bought a play by Jean Jacques Bernard which I found utterly charming, "L'Invitation au Voyage." It is a study in moods more than anything else ; delicate, sensitive, but with no "punch" and very little action. Bernard is one of the leaders among the newer French playwrights ; he is an exponent of the *théorie du silence* ; his plays deal in the overtones, in the poignant, revealing silence of life.

Although one of the few really outstanding failures

of the Civic Repertory Theatre, this play is one of my greatest favorites. Every now and then we say at the theatre, "Let's put in a performance of 'L'Invitation,' " and, amidst black looks from Mrs. Benson and the treasurer of the organization, in it goes ! We play it for our own delight and the very real pleasure of a tiny, faithful audience, people who watch for it carefully to appear on the schedule and come back to it time and again. I call it my luxury. That is another advantage of repertory — one can occasionally indulge in luxuries of that kind !

Our second season opened with "The Good Hope," Heijermans's great drama of the sea. Then followed "2 x 2 = 5" by Wied, and then came the great fun of "Peter Pan."

At last I was to play Peter ; I had looked forward to it for years. Aline Bernstein designed a delightful production full of imagination. It was quite a big undertaking, for the staging is complicated, and then there is dancing and music and fighting and above all *flying!*

When I read the manuscript I had an awful sinking feeling of disappointment on reading stage-directions such as "Peter hides behind the window-curtains, his wire is put on." I had always *believed* so in that flying, and now perforce I must be disillusioned once and for all. As a child I had almost killed myself after seeing "Peter Pan," by mounting the mantelpiece the moment I arrived home and hurling myself to the ground, in an effort to fly across the room. "Peter had done it, so why shouldn't I ?" I thought with my usual arrogance. I sat gazing at my bumps and scratches and decided, "There is more in this flying business than meets the eye" — anyway, from then on I left it to Peter. But now, after all these years, I was to discover Peter's secret.

I found that the Fairy Dust consisted of an extremely elaborate system of wires, counterweights, and pulleys, invented and run for years by the Schultze family. They "flew" Maude Adams during her long run of "Peter Pan" ; they were the originators of the flying ballet in which eighty girls suddenly whirled gaily from the stage of the Hippodrome into the second balcony and back again ; their flying stories are many and fascinating. My first flying lesson was called about a month before the opening, for it takes sometimes ten days to learn, and it is well to have a little practice before tackling the Peter "flies," some of which are quite tricky. The harness that you have to wear through the whole play weighs at least ten pounds and at first is very uncomfortable. The back of it is composed of a solid leather plaque with a brass attachment into which the end of the wire fits. A professional "flying lady" came to give us lessons. She took all sorts of wonderful attitudes in the air, like a ballet dancer, and as we were hauled up one by one, we felt (and probably looked) like bags of flour, helpless and shapeless. Gradually you get the trick, and then what fun it is ! It really gives you the *feeling* of flying. Be-

fore each performance we have to rehearse every one of
the flies, to be sure things are clear aloft on the gridiron,
and that all is in order ; but even so, there is always a
possibility of surprises.   One time little Michael could
not quite get through the window — his wire was not let
out to sufficient length.   Knowing that the pull to the
counterbalance would take him back into the room
straight into the arms of Mrs. Darling, who at that moment was bemoaning his loss, Wendy — who flies just
ahead of him — caught his hand through the window
and pulled the window-curtain around him, and the poor
little boy clung there to the window-frame, hidden by
the curtain, till the end of the scene.

Another afternoon, on Wendy's fly in the second scene,
where Tootles shoots the "Wendy Bird" with an arrow,
they flew her so high that the children in the balcony
couldn't see her entire figure, and a loud voice called
out with appalled interest "He shot her head off !" much
to the delight of the rest of the audience.

Some of the remarks the children make at matinée
performances are terribly funny and at times disconcert-
ing.   They see everything and are keenly critical.   On
our first Saturday afternoon, in the underground scene
when Peter lies asleep on the bed and is awakened by
Tinker Bell's knock on the door, the stage manager, instead of using the floor to make the sound of the knock
on, used the same hollow piece of wood that makes the
tic-tac of the Crocodile.   He happened to have it in his

hand and tapped it with his knuckle. Instantly from
the front of the house a loud voice cried "The crocodile !"
The child's ear had at once recognized the particular
timbre of that piece of wood.

Often when I sit on the barrel in the ship scene, playing the pipes, and Captain Hook creeps up behind me
sword in hand, from all over the house come voices
raised to a squeak of suspense and excitement : "Peter !
Look out, Peter !"   One day a tiny little boy in the front
row stood up and hammered on his seat crying, "Oh,
Peter, Peter, Peter *Pan* !" in an agony of anguish for fear
Hook should get me.

But nothing ever equals the audience at the free
Christmas matinée of "Peter" which we give once a year.
On this occasion the children are completely uninhibited,
for they are almost entirely without the control of grown-
ups.   Also, many of them have never before seen any
sort of entertainment and the whole thing is completely
real to them.   None of us will ever forget the first of
these matinées.   The children did not know ordinary
applause, and they simply *yelled* their approval.   In the
underground scene that afternoon the entire house
shouted out : "Wake up, old Peter !   Somebody wake
him up !   Peter, wake up !"   They kept it up until on
Tinker Bell's knock I went over to the medicine glass
in which Hook had poured the poison.   There the cry
changed to, "Don't touch that glass !"

When Tink is dying and Peter goes to the footlights
crying out, "She says she thinks she can get well again if

children believed in fairies. Do you believe in fairies ?
Say *quick* that you believe ! *If you believe* clap your
hands !" Hand-clapping was not enough for them —
they screamed, "Yes ! Yes ! we believe ! we believe !" in
a frenzy of anxious excitement. Never has Tink been
saved as she was that day !

In the ship scene when Peter yelled, "Down, boys, and
at 'em !" it was pandemonium ! The children hopped
up and down in their seats , some of them jumped up and
ran down the aisles in a wild effort to help us conquer the
pirates ; and when Peter finally jumped on the barrel
and with a mighty blow felled Hook to the ground, the
cheers that went up stopped the show for three minutes.
I have never heard such a noise inside a theatre.

We were all complete wrecks after the performance !
It was so hard not to break down and cry, the response
was so touchingly genuine. Every year we look forward
to this matinée, at which everyone in the theatre gives his
or her services as a present to the "kids." But the "kids"
give us back something we shall all our lives remember
with a warm glow.

After we had been playing "Peter" for some time and I
was considered an expert flyer, I persuaded the Schultzes
to rig up an "audience fly" for me. I thought it would
be much better fun for the children out front (and for
me !) if instead of taking a regular bow in front of the
curtain, I should suddenly fly out to the balcony and
back, so that their last glimpse of Peter would be in the
air.

The first time I rehearsed this "fly" I confess I was a tiny bit scared, but afterwards I grew crazy about it, and of course the effect on the children need not be described. I can see their faces as I swing towards the balcony. At first they are so startled and amazed that they stand up open-mouthed and some even stretch out their hands to catch me, then on the flight back they begin to shout !

One day as I started off, a tall gentleman with a completely bald head, not suspecting my flight, stood up in the centre aisle ; I passed about a foot above him and felt like alighting on his shiny head as I do on the mushroom in the second scene. He sat down very quickly as if he guessed my wicked thoughts.

After the performance there are nearly always several children who come backstage asking to shake hands with Peter Pan and Wendy ; Miss Hutchinson and I usually wait a few minutes before starting to take off our make-up, so the children won't be disillusioned. The great question, especially from little boys over seven is : "How do you fly ?" "Show us how to fly !" I remind them of the "Fairy Dust," but some are old enough to look rather sceptical, though at the same time it is a great mystery. The most amusing solution was offered by one child who had apparently pondered deeply over the problem : "I know ! You take a great swallow of gas and then go up in the air like a balloon !"

One of the "greatest" children we ever entertained backstage was Mr. Mei Lang Fang, the famous Chinese

The Civic Repertory Theatre

"Masha" in "The Sea Gull"   "Marguerite Gautier" in "Camille"
"Peter Pan"   "Juliet" in "Romeo and Juliet"

actor. He was fascinated by the performance, and the flying especially delighted him. We kept the flying crew on and showed him how it was done. I flew from one side of the stage to the other and he stood below with a radiant face, clapping his hands. I had a feeling he was longing to try it himself. He was such a darling ; like all great people, simple and alive with genuine enthusiasm.

One little boy, Freddy, who lives quite near the theatre and has made friends with us all, has seen Peter thirty-eight times and knows every word of it by heart. An amusing scene took place in my dressing-room one day after the matinée. Freddy was there, and a little boy called Roger, the nephew of a friend of mine, came back-stage with a little girl whom he had invited to see the play. Roger had seen Peter three times and was very proud of it. He brought me the gift of a piece of soap which he had painfully carved into the semblance of a turtle. He met Freddy and, with an eye to impress him as well as the little girl, he announced loudly that this was the third time he had seen "Peter Pan." Freddy at once shouted, "Only three times ! Huh ! I've seen it thirty-eight !" There was a dreadful silence ; the little girl cast wondering eyes on Freddy and Roger looked gloomy and crestfallen. After they had gone, Freddy said reflectively, "Only three times !"

Then, feeling that perhaps he had been cruel in crowing too much, and wanting to soften the blow, he stretched out his hand toward the carved soap that lay on my dressing-table and said magnanimously : "Still, that was a beautiful turtle he made !"

But it would be easy to fill a book with stories of "Peter Pan." It is one of the most popular bills in our repertory, both with the public and with the company. Every year we look forward to getting back to it. I think no children enjoy it any more than we do !

IT was during our second season that I was awarded the *Pictorial Review* Prize for 1926. It was a very great honor and made me very happy. Mother was staying with me that winter and came to the big dinner given on the occasion. It was an impressive business. I felt quite overwhelmed, there were so many important, interesting people there. Mr. Kahn presided and made one of his delightful speeches. It made me feel shy and rather ashamed to hear so many wonderful things said about me, I was called "gallant," "courageous," "an un-selfish leader in the American Theatre" ; I was praised to the skies for the "great sacrifice" I had made "in the interest of the Drama" ; it was all so bewildering !

In my speech of thanks I tried to make clear the fact that I had been completely and utterly *selfish ;* I had done what I wanted to do, the way I wanted to do it. There could be no question of abnegation : I had never had so much fun in my life ! Hard work ? Yes ! But wasn't that what I had been clamoring for for years ? Courageous ! Is it courageous to do a thing in *ignorance* of fear ? Had I been less ignorant I *might* have been afraid. I had walked in, like a child, where angels feared to tread ! However I felt enormously grateful and the $5,000 came in very handy ! My one hope was that some day the work of our theatre would justify the high hopes that had prompted such a signal honor as that now bestowed on the Civic Repertory Company.

Our third season was a particularly brilliant and exciting one. The great actress Alla Nazimova had decided to join us and was to appear in Tchekov's "The Cherry Orchard" and Andreyev's "Katerina." Since first seeing Madame Nazimova play in " 'Ception Shoals" shortly after my arrival in this country, I had been one of her most ardent admirers, and now the thought of working with her filled me with delight.

We all felt a little trepidation at having such a famous star among us. Would she be temperamental ? Would she be "upstage" ? How would she behave ? We need have had no fear ! No one could have been simpler, more warm-hearted, enthusiastic, and utterly charming. She won everyone's heart and within a few days we all thought of her as a comrade. And what a splendid worker she is ! It was indeed an inspiration to act with her. She is indefatigable in her search for just the right touch, the right nuance. She is never satisfied, never pleased with herself ; always looking forward to playing "better the next time." And with it all, such a sense of fun ! Nothing highbrow or smug about *her* ! Just a delightful human being and a great artist.

It was during our third season that I started the Apprentice Group. I had always felt that in connection with a repertory theatre there should be a school. But it should not be the ordinary dramatic academy, and above all, it should be *free*.

My idea was to take some thirty or forty young boys and girls, chosen through auditions, and accept them as apprentices to the work of the theatre. There was to be no tuition fee whatever. The only actual courses they would receive were fencing, dancing, speech and make-up. They would be in intimate touch with a repertory theatre working at full speed, would be allowed to watch rehearsals, and occasionally take part as supers in productions which involved big ensemble scenes. They themselves were to work on material which they could choose, and give performances on the stage before the members of the company, who would help them with criticism and advice. After each of their productions I would spend several hours with them, giving my impressions of their work, and answering any questions they wanted to put before me. The greatest advantage seemed to me to lie in the possibilities for observation and study open to them. If they had talent, they would know instinctively how to make use of the chances put before them.

We were swamped with applications. So many young people seem to be bitten with the theatre "bug" ! Some have real talent, others are attracted by the glamour, others again are lazy and think of acting as a quick and easy way of making vast sums of money. It is tremen-

dously hard to weed them out.   The auditions are a real
problem.   One wants so desperately to be fair ; it is impossible to go by outward appearance ; sometimes those
who seem the most uncouth and awkward prove to be
real finds, while a young man with a fine easy manner, a
good voice, and a handsome face turns out a total loss.
It is necessary to try to sense their *inner* quality.   One
tries to catch by surprise some trace of sensibility or imagination, humor, or aspiration — some rare quality that
springs unconsciously from their very centre.

Poor children, they look upon the audition as an ordeal.   If they only knew what an ordeal it is for me !

Only a few months ago I gave the auditions for the
coming season.   I sat for two weeks, four days a week
from ten A.M. till six P.M. concentrating and racking my
brains and feelings in an effort to see clearly.   I gave
nearly six hundred individual hearings and chose nearly
fifty students.   Some of that number will in all probability be eliminated during the first months of the
season.

Mrs. Edward Bok, whose marvelous work with the
Curtis Institute is so well known, has taken a great interest in the Civic Repertory Theatre.   Among the many
helpful things she has done to further our work is her
donation of a scholarship fund, enabling four of the most
talented apprentices to stay on a second year with our
theatre ; during this second year they are sometimes
allowed to play bits and to understudy.

The plan has worked out remarkably well.   And it has

been interesting and stimulating. During the season of
1932–33 there were five young members of the company who had worked up from various apprentice groups
during the preceding few years.

On many occasions, I must confess, we have all wished
the students far, far away ! They are an undisciplined,
selfish, arrogant lot as a rule, but they are so young ; and
if out of fifty you find one who *really* has something, it's
worth while putting up with the rest of them !

The fourth season we added our third Tchekov play
to the repertory : "The Sea Gull." I took the small but
very interesting part of Masha ; this was the third of
Tchekov's women wearing black that I had played.
Masha in "The Three Sisters" and Varya in "The
Cherry Orchard" were the other two. Just as in painting there is a note of black somewhere on the canvas, so
Tchekov in his plays has nearly always that note of
black in one of his female characters. It seems to bring
the other figures into relief in a curious way ; from a
director's angle it is immensely intriguing ; of course it
is true, too, that the wearing of black is an outward
manifestation of an inner state of mind, especially when
worn by young women, and these three women of
Tchekov's are all quite young. I think "The Sea Gull"
is perhaps the most difficult of all his plays. In it, even
more than in the others, it is a matter of catching a
mood, particularly in the first act. We worked terribly
hard on it.

But the production I enjoyed most of all, and on which

I think I worked the hardest was "Romeo and Juliet."
During the summer, out in the country, I had planned
to prepare "As You Like It," which I intended adding to
the repertory for the fourth season ; but try as I would
to concentrate on it, "Romeo and Juliet" kept creeping
into my thoughts. I became obsessed by it and finally
gave in and substituted it for "As You Like It" in the
schedule of productions. I had seen it played twice,
but had never liked the way it was done. It had always
seemed to me to lack tempo, warmth, and youth.

I wanted our production to give a sense of the Italy
of that period ; it should be colorful, violent, and above
all *swift*. There should be no scene-waits, the whole
story should flow without interruption and increasing in
tempo and suspense till the final curtain. For it is after
all, an awfully exciting story ; it is not just a lyrical "love-
fest." To my mind the play is too often treated as a
star vehicle, which robs it of its broader canvas, like looking at a detail in a painting and missing the meaning and
drama of the *whole*.

Together Mrs. Bernstein and I solved the technical
problems of the production. I went directly to Shakespeare's text, to find out as nearly as possible what he had
visualized. His directions for the farewell scene are :
"Romeo and Juliet appear above at the window" ; as a
rule the scene is played in the bedroom and is extremely
unconvincing. In his text, the last scene is played "in a
graveyard in which stands a monument belonging to the
Capulets" ; though as a rule the scene is played in the

tomb itself. What he asks for is in every case infinitely more dramatic, but (provided, of course, one doesn't use the typical Elizabethan stage, discarding all scenery), it demands a certain amount of ingenuity in the staging, which with the marvelous scenic-equipment now at our command is comparatively simple.

It is by far the most fascinating production I have ever worked on. Now that our repertory was fairly well stocked and very flexible, we were able to give ten weeks to rehearsals of "Romeo and Juliet." I wanted to use the Tschaikovsky music, and, being unable to afford the large orchestra it really requires, I called for help to my old friend David Mannes, and he proved a friend indeed ! He took time out of his busy life to spend many hours at our theatre and somehow, with a couple of added instruments, managed to make our little orchestra play the difficult music very commendably.

Many times during the final dress rehearsals, I couldn't help dreaming of how wonderful it would be if I were able to spend money lavishly ; to have twenty trumpeters instead of two ; an orchestra of fifty instead of one of seven ; a hundred supers instead of fifteen ! Still, it is better to be forced to make a great deal out of a very little. It keeps one's imagination and sense of invention working at top speed ; it is fun to overcome difficulties.

We played this production first in Philadelphia. There, as later in New York, it was received with extraordinary enthusiasm. To my great joy we had managed to make the play exciting and alive, and people were carried away by the vitality of the splendid old story. They forgot that it was "Shakespeare" and sat on the edge of their seats following the action with breathless interest.

I had paid careful attention to the fight scenes, which were staged by the great fencing-master, Professor Santelli. The duel between Tybalt and Mercutio, ending in Mercutio's death, was really thrilling ; the company used to crowd in the wings every performance to watch it. There was no make-believe "stage-fight" about it ; every move, every thrust was genuine ; it was almost terrifying in its reality.

And what a delight it was to speak those magnificent lines ! The sheer beauty of them was intoxicating. Sometimes, during periods of particularly hard work in the theatre, I felt very tired and thought I should *never* be able to play — almost dreaded it, in fact ; but the moment I started Juliet's magical phrases, I felt carried away from the stress of ordinary surroundings into another world. I had thought that the fact of speaking verse would perhaps prove a handicap, would give one a sense of constraint ; I found the contrary to be true : these lines seemed to bring one greater breadth, greater freedom.

During that engagement in Philadelphia an amusing incident happened ; it is a definite proof of the value of "ensemble" playing through repertory experience. Our business had been so splendid that we were obliged to give a special matinée and chose for that extra bill a little comedy by the Quinteros : "The Women Have Their Way," which was one of the five plays included in the Philadelphia season. The first act works up to one of the funniest scenes of the comedy, in which six women sit gossiping endlessly, with fans and tongues working at full speed. It occurs just after the entrance of Juanita, the heroine, and her aunt. Their arrival has been worked up by the other ladies who, seeing them from a distance, prepare to receive them in a flutter of anticipation, for there is gossip afoot about Juanita and a certain young man from Madrid and they are longing to see how she and her aunt will react.

I stood in the wings, in my Juanita make-up, waiting for my cue, which was near ; I looked round for my "aunt" and found to my surprise that she was nowhere to be seen. As a rule she was extremely punctual and was ready at the entrance well ahead of her cue. I called the stage manager and asked him to go to her room and warn her that it was almost time to go on. He returned with a flushed, horrified face and informed me she was not in the theatre !

There was scarcely a moment in which to decide on any special action — no way of communicating our plight to the people on the stage ; they went gaily on talking of the "aunt," suspecting nothing. Then came my cue and with a beating heart, but outwardly calm and smiling, I stepped onto the stage, *alone !*

I shall never forget their faces ! I managed to whisper to Miss Hutchinson and Miss Mooney, who were the first

to greet me, that so far as I knew there would be no
"aunt" and we should have to carry on as best we could.
Miss Ward started off by asking "Where is your aunt?
I thought I saw her coming with you?"   To which I very
truthfully replied : "No, she stayed at home !"

Then the fun began.   It was like a fast game of ball.
We had to divide her lines, some of which were very important, among the five of us ; in some cases lines had to
be altered to fit the new situation.   This was miraculously accomplished ; none of us spoke at the same time,
there was no confusion, there seemed to be a sort of
mental telepathy between us.   We "got over" all the
laughs, the scene went as swiftly and surely as if we had
always played it that way.   The audience had no idea
there was anything wrong, and the applause at the end
of the act was as enthusiastic as usual.

When the curtain fell we were all shaking with nerves
and excitement.   Though during the ordeal we had
been as cool as cucumbers, when it was over I confess my
knees felt extremely weak !

Thank God we were at last able to produce "the aunt"
in the second act !   She had been found at her hotel,
blissfully unconscious of the fact that a special matinée
had been called.   She had misread the call board, but
fortunately had not decided on a trip to Atlantic City for
the day !   I don't know whether we could have sustained
another whole act of such mental gymnastics !

I doubt if such a feat could have been carried off in
an ordinary company.   It was simply the fact of our

being so used to one another's rhythm, so used to playing together in so many varied plays, to helping each
other out in a hundred different situations, that had
stood us in good stead in this emergency, which might
otherwise have turned out very differently.

OUR first new production the following season was
Giraudoux's remarkable play, "Siegfried." I was very
much disappointed at the reception given to it. A few
people felt it was the best thing we had so far presented,
but the majority found it "talky" and dull. It certainly
is a play that requires listening to, but what it has to say
is worth that small effort, it seems to me.

As an American citizen, I suppose I have a right to
criticize our country now and then, and I do feel that
as audiences we are apt to be unpardonably lazy. We
are too prone to demand labor-saving devices in our
mental as well as our physical activities. The French are
of course an ardently cerebral race ; they delight in the
purely intellectual, in the discussion of abstract problems. It may be for this reason that as a general rule the
modern French Theatre, with its growing tendency
towards difficult and sometimes obscure psychological
subjects, is not particularly successful in America. The
conciseness, the precision of the French language is, to
begin with, extremely hard to translate, and with us
conversation for conversation's sake is a dying art ; it does
not interest us to listen to a mere exchange of ideas no
matter how original or arresting they may be.

"Mirandolina" in "La
   Locandiera"

"Ella Rentheim" in "John
   Gabriel Borkman"

"Dorimène" in "The Would-be
   Gentleman"

"Hilda Wangel" in "The Master
   Builder"

"Camille"

Our fifth season was also interesting through our production of Susan Glaspell's "Alison's House." It was cruelly treated by the press, well received by the public — and to our great jubilation — was awarded the Pulitzer Prize for 1931.

Then came the greatest popular success the Civic Repertory Theatre has ever known : "Camille."

I was very tired and fell ill with bronchitis during rehearsals. I played a matinée of "Peter Pan" with a temperature of one hundred and three. That night I put an understudy in "The Cradle Song," and went to bed. It was a difficult business. The following week I crawled out and struggled through "Alison's House" once, then had to give up. I was terribly worried about rehearsals of "Camille," which was to open in two weeks.

By a great stroke of luck Constance Collier had just finished work on her production of "Peter Ibbetson," and I sent her a wild call for help. She was marvelous ; I don't know what we should have done without her ! She took over the rehearsals, the entire direction of the play. An understudy read my lines and I lay in bed working as best I could on the part. Fortunately I knew the play thoroughly and had mapped out pretty well what I wanted to do with Marguerite. Miss Collier gave me her usual clear, inspiring criticism during my three days of actual work on the stage, and after these three dress rehearsals I was ready to open. A doctor stood in the wings and gave me treatments between the acts, for I had great difficulty in breathing. To my relief the old

play went over magnificently, and the evening was an exciting and happy one for us all.

I used the original Dumas text with scarcely a change ;
it was excellently translated by Henriette Metcalf. We
simply eliminated the monologues either by cutting or
by other devices. I set the play in the 1870's, for I
wanted to use the "Traviata" score to heighten the
glamour of the action. If you are going to play "La
Dame aux Camélias" it must be played for all it's worth,
with as much magic as possible and a certain amount of
bravura, and I felt the music of "Traviata" would serve
to underline these qualities in the production.

We have never turned more people away than on
"Camille" nights. The play is based on fundamental
human emotions that never grow old. I think the best
description of it was given by Henry James when he
wrote :

"Written by Dumas when he was twenty-five, 'Camille' remains in its combination of freshness and form and of the feeling of the springtime of life, a singular, an astonishing piece
of work. The novel and the play have been blown about the
world at a fearful rate, but the story has never lost its happy
juvenility, a charm that nothing can vulgarize. It is all cham-
pagne and tears — fresh perversity, fresh credulity, fresh passion, fresh pain. We have seen the play both well done and ill
done — in strange places, in barbarous tongues. But nothing
makes any difference — it carries with it an April air : some
tender young man and some coughing young woman have only

to speak the lines to give it a great place among the love-stories of the world."

I have never felt so tired as during the last months of that season. The five years of grilling work, incessant responsibility, and worry were beginning to tell on me, my illness had left me very weak and with no chance of rest I could not seem to regain my strength.

I came to a drastic decision : I would take a year off for rest and study. My battery was running very low, and I wanted a chance to recharge it with fresh energy. I felt it would be of no use to stick it out, doing mediocre work lacking in vitality ; our work *must* go forward, otherwise there was no reason for our existing. It was imperative for me to go away, to get a new perspective on my job, and turn over quietly in my mind the many things which my first five years had taught me.

Again friends warned me, saying that my announcement would be misconstrued ; people would think I was giving up ; that the Civic Repertory had failed, or that I had grown tired of it and was off to Hollywood ! I merely replied they could think what they liked, I was only doing what I had to do. Furthermore we were closing on the greatest success we had ever had ; the theatre had been packed, our percentage of attendance had grown in the five years from forty-six percent to ninety-one percent of capacity, and this certainly did not imply failure. As to my going to Hollywood, they would find out I had no such intention, and that's all there was to that !

Our closing week we gave all our most popular plays. Every performance was completely sold out : they were "The Master Builder," "The Cradle Song," "Romeo and Juliet," "Peter Pan," "Camille" ; and we had the great happiness of having Mme. Nazimova rejoin us for two performances of "The Cherry Orchard."

For the closing performance we played "Camille." That evening we shall none of us forget. We were all moved to tears by the genuine affection that seemed to come to us from across the footlights. My heart was so full I could scarcely speak my good-bye to all our friends out there who had supported us so consistently and loyally. I could only express our warm thanks, and the hope that we would find them all there again in 1932.

And so our First Five Years were over. They had been wonderful, thrilling years, full of struggles, hard work, patience, endurance, and much happiness !

It would be impossible for me adequately to write of my immense gratitude for the co-operation, faith, and affectionate loyalty shown me by every member of the Civic Repertory organization. People talk of "my" achievement ! Where should I have been without *them ?* They worked with unceasing energy, with magnificent confidence, and in a spirit of unselfish comradeship that overcame obstacles at first sight overwhelming.

In these five years we had produced thirty-four plays, of which I personally directed thirty-two. I had had op-

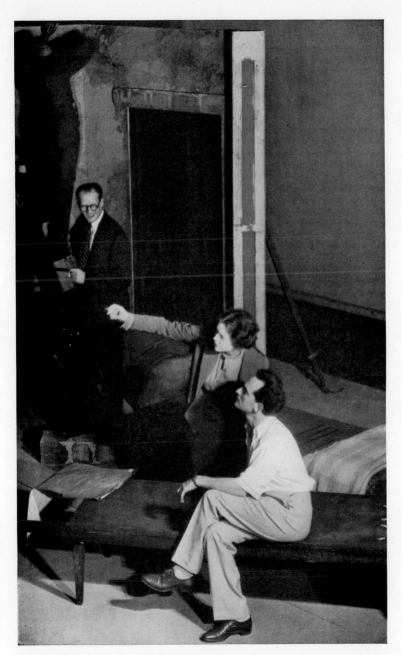

A rehearsal at the Civic Repertory

Eva Le Gallienne, M.A., Litt.D., D.H.L.

portunities to develop both as an actress and as a producer ; the wide range of our program brought us in touch with every type of play, every type of character. No training could have been more thorough. I felt that given the opportunity to go away from the theatre for a year, all that I had learned would gradually sift through my consciousness and become clear and definite. I needed a year of dreams, a chance to get acquainted once more with my inner self.

It was not many weeks after the closing that I found out just *why* I had been so insistent on giving way to my impulse to rest. In an explosion at my house in the country I was badly injured and in any case would have been unable to work for a year. The first thing I thought of on coming to in the hospital was "Thank God ! Everything has been arranged for the theatre to remain closed next season !" My accident would change no one's plans but my own. It turned a year of rest into a year of pain.

I suppose there must be some reason for things like that, though at the time we can't see it. We only see a fragment of the pattern, which often looks ugly and grotesquely wrong. If we could see the whole we would understand just how it all fits in.

Through this accident I at least learned two things : what real suffering is and how *kind* people are. They are good things to know. I realized that it is quite impossible to *imagine* agony ; you may *think* you can, but you have to go through it yourself to really know.

I was overwhelmed at the amazing goodness shown to me. All over the country people seemed to be sending me kind thoughts ; I'm sure they helped me through an ordeal that had somehow cut my life in two.

I felt that I was starting all over again ; as though I stood on the threshold of a *new* life.

XIII

In the summer of 1932, I felt ready to work again. My hands, so wrecked by the accident the previous summer, had been miraculously mended by that great surgeon, Dr. John J. Moorhead ; the man who had, as I always like to say, "put Fred Stone together again." He is not only a great doctor, but a great human being as well. His humor tempered by understanding, his wit tempered by tenderness, add an hundredfold to his genius as a surgeon. I felt that I was not only in the hands of a great medical man, but had also met a friend to whom forever my loyalty and gratitude will remain unchanging.

Our sixth season, on which I had been working during my year of so-called rest, was to include a revival of "Liliom" ; a new American play based on Jane Austen's life — "Dear Jane" ; a production of "Alice in Wonderland" ; one of Galsworthy's plays, "Loyalties" ; and Bottomley's fine poetic drama on the youth of Macbeth and his lady, "Gruach."

It seemed to me inconceivable to play "Liliom" without Joseph Schildkraut. Fortunately he entered into the idea wholeheartedly and agreed to join our company to play not only his original part in the Molnar play, but also Armand in "Camille," Sir John Evelyn in "Dear Jane," Ferdinand de Levis in "Loyalties," Romeo in "Romeo and Juliet," the Queen of Hearts in "Alice in Wonderland" ; and other parts in our repertory.

Ten years had passed since we played together in the first production of "Liliom" presented by the Theatre Guild. We had both changed, and we agreed that the change had been for the better ! I was less pigheaded, less arrogant ; my sense of humor had improved, as well as my patience, and the somewhat pedantic way of thinking and feeling that was objectionable in my salad days had, to a great extent, lightened under the stress of many difficult years of work, involving as they did the thousand human contacts and problems that an actor-manager must fall heir to.

As to "Pepi" Schildkraut, he had come to realize that temper does not necessarily mean temperament, and that fiendish manners are not the only true sign of the great artist ! He genuinely loved the Theatre, and the influence of his father, a truly fine actor, was more and more evident in his approach to his work. We laughed a lot, recalling our absurd ways of ten years back. No one could have been more enthusiastic or more helpful. We went to work joyfully on the play that had done so much for us both in our early days.

It was a strange experience returning to Julie after such a long absence. This part in which I had had to work so hard at twenty-two in order now and then to force emotion to break through, at thirty-three offered

the entirely opposite problem : I had to work with all
my might to control and keep back the emotion that insistently demanded expression, but to which Julie could
never have given free reign.   She was too mute, too repressed, too humble, to allow her inner life and suffering
to appear on the surface.   But the poignancy and force
of her pain, coming in contact with my heightened development as a human being and my greater understanding of what Stanislavsky calls the "technique of emotion," forced me to use great restraint where previously
I had had to goad my feelings on.

We played a short road engagement before opening
in New York at our old theatre.   While playing "Liliom"
and "Camille" on tour, we also rehearsed "Dear Jane"
and "Alice in Wonderland."

I had worked for over a year on the problem of translating the immortal Alice to the stage ; a problem that I
well knew to be fraught with danger.   I had visions of
the irate lovers of Lewis Carroll's masterpiece turning on
me and tearing me limb from limb in blind rage, accus-
ing me of desecrating their sacred heritage.   There is an
element of fanaticism in people's appreciation or non-
appreciation of this bewildering and brilliant book.   I
decided to base our production on my firm conviction
that "Alice in Wonderland" is by no means primarily for
children.   I am indeed inclined to believe the opposite
to be true.   The reaction of the public and the critics
conclusively proved me right.

From what I had heard of other productions here and

elsewhere, the tendency had been to create a sort of pantomime (in the English sense of the word) exclusively for children. The pretty, the cute, the loathesomely whimsical had dominated the scheme. In the text that Miss Friebus and I eventually evolved there was not one word that was not Carroll. For practical purposes some of the incidents were changed in sequence, but in sequence only. Some incidents had to be eliminated, since, as everyone knows, the audience will stand a performance lasting four or five hours only if it be presented by the Guild and the author be Eugene O'Neill. Otherwise two hours and twenty minutes is the time-limit.

I felt that two things were of paramount importance : first, the visual aspect of the production ; secondly, the dream quality, which could be established only by continuous action, with Alice never leaving the stage ; for in one's own dream, one is always present.

The first of these two problems was easily solved ; everyone thinks of "Alice in Wonderland" pictorially in terms of Tenniel's drawings. The second problem was more difficult, for obviously the play, like the book, falls into many short scenes or episodes. The technical solution of this problem was fascinating to me ; I have always adored overcoming obstacles.

I finally evolved a scheme through which it was possible to make the action continuous by the use of a track laid horizontally across the stage upon which two medium-sized chariot platforms alternately rode, shuttlewise, varied occasionally by the use of the full stage without platform, and backed by a roll of scenery that could, if necessary, be kept in constant motion at varying speeds. Instead of Alice's having to leave the stage and go from one environment to another, she remained upon the stage and the various environments came to her and surrounded her. This gave a curious effect of her being in a dream where "things flow about so."

To imagine a difficult technical production in one's mind, and to realize it on the stage of a theatre in flesh and blood and scenery, are two very different things. The attempt at such realization to anyone who loves and knows the Theatre is the most thrilling, terrifying, and breath-taking of experiences. Will it work? Will it be right? How much can one translate from dream to reality? The ten weeks before the production of "Alice in Wonderland" were incredibly exciting. I shall never forget the first time we saw those platforms move!

Certainly no producer ever had more amazing cooperation. Anyone coming in from outside would have thought we were all escaped lunatics. And we were lunatics, but not "escaped"; we were captured, haunted, obsessed, living in a mad world beyond the Looking Glass.

Our playing schedule, after we opened on October 26th with "Liliom," had been very heavy. The repertory included (besides "Liliom") "Camille," "The Cradle Song," "The Three Sisters," "Peter Pan," and a new play "Dear Jane," a charming comedy by Eleanor H. Hinkley.

I had allowed six full-dress rehearsals for "Alice in Wonderland," which was to open December 12th. There were innumerable details to work out. The young art director, Irene Sharaff, was in full charge of minutely reproducing the Tenniel drawings. She succeeded in doing a difficult job astonishingly well. Remo Bufano worked on masks and marionettes. The actors, who during rehearsals had had full use of their own faces and bodies, suddenly, at the first dress rehearsal, found themselves coping with the amazing articulated masks and weird costumes, and everything seemed on the verge of tragic catastrophe. Gallantly they rallied and grew accustomed to a different form of expression, learning to handle and overcome the handicaps that faithfulness to Tenniel imposed upon them.

We had the great joy of having at many of our rehearsals Clemence Dane, who between lectures would return to New York and, fortunately for us, adopted the Civic Repertory Theatre as a frequent camping ground. Her warm enthusiasm, her keen criticism, her marvelous sense of the Theatre were invaluable to us in keeping up our morale and freshening our sense of values.

It was through Miss Dane that I was lucky enough to discover Richard Addinsell, whose witty music did much to heighten the production of "Alice." He had composed the music for Miss Dane's play, "Adam's Opera," which, strangely enough, has not yet been presented in America.

Clemence Dane is a rare and extraordinary person.

When one thinks that one woman wrote "A Bill of Divorcement," "Granite," "Legend," "Will Shakespeare," "Adam's Opera," "Broome Stages," and "Wild December" (to mention only a few of her works) the range of her mind and the sweep of her understanding amaze one. As a person, she is simple, direct, vital, imbued with an incorrigible interest in every phase of life, every kind of person ; brilliant, sane, a veritable dynamo of energy, always eager to help, never thinking of herself as the great artist she so truly is, without affectation or pose of any kind, a thorough and magnificent worker.

The rehearsals during the daytime over, we played our show at night, whatever it might be, and then the technical staff went on. I don't suppose any of us had more than three hours' sleep a night for at least ten days before the opening.

These night rehearsals were a bedlam. On the fore stage Miss Wilton would be desperately trying to make the front and back legs of the horse agree. At the piano, Mr. Addinsell, patiently playing over and over again the entrance of the White Knight, the owner of the horse.

In the background, Mr. Bufano and his assistants, working on the choreography of the Walrus and the Carpenter, super-marionettes. Up on the bridge, several of our students learning to control the many oysters that were to succumb to the blandishments of the wicked Walrus and the cold-blooded Carpenter.

Myself in the middle section of the stage working with Miss Chandler, our stage manager, and with Ralph

Phillips, Henry Linck, and Joe Roig (carpenter, electrician, and property man respectively), perfecting the technical elements of the scenery, trying out one thing and another until we hit on something that seemed best ; then running over to supervise the latest development of the horse or the oysters.

A stretched-out figure on one side of the stage, seemingly a corpse — Mr. Richard Waring, his whole face covered in plaster of Paris, having a new mask made for the White Rabbit, his first having been unsuccessful.

Miss Sharaff, adjusting the Mouse's tummy, which seemed to have slipped a bit.

Miss Hutchinson patiently placing the ladder against the horse's side so that Mr. Da Silva, the White Knight, could mount his steed, by this time more or less synchronized in its legs by Miss Wilton's and Mr. Addinsell's efforts.

What an amazing and ludicrous series of snapshots come into mind at the thought of these rehearsals ! And how marvelous all the people were ! Their enthusiasm, patience, fortitude, gaiety, and faith are unforgettable. Without such perfect co-operation and help, Alice would never have stepped out of my dream to dream for herself on the stage and — as it happened to our everlasting joy and gratitude — give pleasure to the many thousands of children from six to sixty (and over), as Mr. Garland so happily said, who came to see the play, and to the many other thousands who I hope will come in the future.

"Alice in Wonderland" was a tremendous success. Critics were lavish in their praise of the production, the music, and especially of Miss Hutchinson's uncanny performance as Alice. She had achieved the seemingly impossible feat of becoming everyone's Alice. Alice's looks, her solemnity, her occasional sulkiness, her obstinacy, and her practical, analytical questions, all were there. Miss Hutchinson never fell into the trap, so dangerous for an adult artist playing a child, of becoming cute or unbearably whimsical, or striving to look and behave like "seven and a half exactually." She just *was*.

Her greatest tributes came from the children themselves. I remember one marvelous letter I had from a young man of six who wanted my picture and one of Alice. He added a P. S. saying : "Listen, Eva ! Mother says Alice is a lady ; *I* think she's a little girl !"

Letters came to Miss Hutchinson from many a little "Wendy" girl asking anxiously if she had a mother to take her home and give her some dinner ; otherwise, she was to have dinner with them. They were anxious and worried at the thought that she was there, surrounded by strange and unkind animals, chess-queens, cards, and other monsters.

Speaking of animals, the pig — Phoebe, for some reason ! — was one of our great pets. She was perfectly tame and seemed a natural actress. She performed for the last two months without her leash, went on the stage at her proper cue and ran off again at the right moment and to the right spot, where her bottle of warmed milk awaited her. She then ran to the property room, climbed into her traveling box and was taken in a taxi to her home at the veterinary. She is at this moment grunting outside my window. She has grown into a large sow of handsome proportions, but, of course, anyone who has taken a part in "Alice in Wonderland" could never *never* become sausage or bacon, so she is leading an idyllic life in Westport, Connecticut, resting on her past laurels.

If "Alice" had not been a success, I really think I should have been dreadfully unhappy. So much hope and faith and sincere love had gone into the making of it ; so many good workers would have been broken-hearted. But God and the critics were good to us, and at the most difficult moment in the history of the Civic Repertory Theatre, it at least had the asset of one of the biggest box-office draws in New York.

We had indeed arrived at a difficult moment, one might almost say an insurmountable barrier. I have already explained that the basic idea of our theatre was non-commercial. With our comparatively small capacity at our very low prices, striving to keep to as high a standard of production as possible, it was, of course, out of the question to make any profit or even to make expenses. We were definitely dependent in our present situation on the faith of a few wealthy patrons who felt as we did about the value of our particular type of theatre in the community.

Josephine Hutchinson as "Alice" in "Alice in Wonderland"

The Trial Scene in "Alice in Wonderland"

Our intake at the box office had climbed to an amazingly high average, but we still needed a subsidy of at
least $75,000 a year to continue our policy and to sustain,
as well, our free school.

With the disaster of the depression, several of our
financial backers found themselves literally unable to
help. I was faced with a new situation, and a drastic decision was forced upon me. A large sum of money on
which I had counted to pay for the production of "Alice
in Wonderland" was unavoidably denied me. On several previous occasions, with "The Cradle Song," "The
Cherry Orchard," "Romeo and Juliet," "Peter Pan,"
"Camille," etc., I had received offers to go uptown. I
had always refused, for to accept would have been incon-
sistent.

I was now faced with a choice between complete defeat
and temporary compromise ; I, who hate compromise almost more than defeat, nevertheless chose this course.

When you are responsible for the livelihood of many
workers and when you feel that by temporary compromise an idea to which you have devoted your life's
thought and many years of intense work can be saved,
and when this idea has been realized through the belief
and unselfish efforts of many people, it seems to me that
is not the time for squeamish and selfish adherence to
pride, or for a blind persistence in an idea at that moment
impossible of execution.

That, in any case, was my feeling ; and, after consult-
ing the company and staff, who magnificently gave me

their whole-hearted co-operation, we moved uptown to the New Amsterdam Theatre with one production, "Alice in Wonderland."

It seemed strange and horrible after six years of repertory to play the same play performance after performance. It was strange to be playing in an alien theatre. We were so used and so devoted to our own funny old house. People have called it shabby, and perhaps it is ; but to us, it was home. We each had our own dressing-room on the level of the stage, and our green-room ; any small improvement in equipment or in personal comfort was examined and appreciated by the whole company. We loved the old house, even to loving its defects ; then, suddenly to play in a theatre as prosperous and coldly well-equipped as the New Amsterdam was frightening and a little gruesome.

Not that we were ungrateful to the New Amsterdam. Of all uptown theatres, I think it is the pleasantest. Its large auditorium, beautifully built and graded, manages somehow to appear intimate. The stage equipment is, of course, excellent, and the dressing-rooms are sumptuous. There is a personal atmosphere about it that suggests its owner to be a lover of the Theatre and of that theatre in particular. It is definitely not a stepchild. It was built and has been preserved with affectionate pride. All of this, however, though we well appreciated it, could not prevent us from feeling strangers in a strange, even though very charming, house.

We were fortunate in being able to secure Mme. Nazimova's co-operation. She consented to join us for some performances of "The Cherry Orchard" and played the first half of the week for five weeks in this play, while "Alice" played the final half. This made us feel a little more at home ; it was after all a move slightly in the direction of our beloved repertory scheme. It was good too to see again Nazimova's brilliant performance as Lubov Andreyevna and to work with her on this great and tender masterpiece, by one of our most loved authors, Tchekov.

So we succeeded, through one of the most difficult seasons on record in the annals of the theatre, in carrying on until May sixth. On that date, I decided to close and meditate upon our next move.

For the first time in many years, I was faced with indecision. From the point of view of opportunities, I certainly could not complain ; I had more offers, more "propositions," than I could have dreamed possible. People felt that my Civic Repertory dream had, of necessity, come to an end, and that I would therefore be open to a good commercial offer, either in the theatre or in pictures ; and these commercial offers, many of them kind and (from a certain standpoint) flattering, were in view of my reputation for "cussedness" couched in idealistic terms. But "cussed" I had been for years, and "cussed" I remain.

Here is the moment, I feel, for a digression into certain evils of the present theatrical scheme.

I believe that the legitimate theatre can and will of

necessity regain its lost importance, but it must revert into the hands of those workers who know it and love it. It must no longer be controlled by real estate and high finance.

These workers fall into eight categories:

1. Manager
2. Actor-Manager
3. Director
4. Actor
5. Playwright
6. Musician
7. Scenic Designer
8. Stage hand

All of these elements, necessary to our modern stage production, should, if they wish to save the Theatre and serve it, work together in complete accord and with the greatest co-operation. This, at the present moment, they do not do. There is too much distrust, too much antagonism and jealousy, and this at a time when the Theatre itself, in its very essence, is in danger.

How can a house divided conquer?

The people who persist in the belief that the "talkies" have annihilated the Theatre can be immediately discounted.

How could such a thing be? The "talkies" in no way conflict with the Theatre. Canned vegetables can never entirely take the place of those picked fresh from the garden. No matter how good the record of a voice, it cannot supplant the living voice itself.

There is an element of surprise about the living performance of a great actor in a great part ; you, as a member of the audience, by your very response or indifference become a factor in the miracle that may happen. This is no product passed upon by several gentlemen of high degree in Hollywood, passed upon again and censored by other gentlemen, expert in morals, sealed in a tin and shipped by express or plane, exhibited at a certain price in a theatre of grandiose dimensions and over-comfortable armchairs to your indifferent approbation !

Whatever that tin may contain will pass before your eyes and din into your ears, and you sit there, impersonal and helpless. What does it matter if you hiss your disapproval and throw rotten eggs ? What does it matter if you stand on your seat and shout your ecstatic approbation ? It is dead. It belongs to the past. There can be from those shadows no response of terror, of shame, or of joy and loving gratitude. Truly the actor as "the servant of the people" has disappeared. A servant is never safe from disapproval — never removed from praise. Neither is an idol.

How can the public ever truly feel that the Theatre, with all its living glamour, could be replaced by an untouchable piece of mechanism ?

No ! It is not from without that the Theatre is in danger ; it is from within.

In the old days, the palmy days of the Theatre, an actor could also be a stage hand, a stage hand could also be a musician, a musician could also be a playwright, and a manager could be actor, musician, playwright, and stage hand combined, provided he was competent for the jobs.

Nowadays, we are all specialists belonging to certain unions and controlled by them. This situation has brought about much good, but also some evils. I think it is unintelligent to be radiantly satisfied with half-solutions.

It is a definite good to have reduced injustice and despotism, in the sense of having made impossible the grueling work at starvation wages frequent before the creation of the Actors' Equity and the musicians', stage hands', and other unions connected with theatrical production.

I think it is a definite evil to make these unions so hide-bound, so drastic, and at times so ludicrous in their petty rules that they become the greatest impediment and obstacle in the path of sincere and honest stage activities. If it were only possible to unite all these elements in a common purpose : the preservation and development of our American Theatre ! If we could only eliminate the antagonism, distrust, and jealousy that unfortunately continue to hamper activity in production, a great end would be achieved.

There should be drastic penalties for those who fall below the accepted standards of fair play, but it seems to me that consistent belief that foul play will be the only possible outcome of any generous concession is a point of view pernicious and destructive to the highest degree.

The workers in the Theatre, of all categories, should and must get together (possibly under a general and impartial leader) to save the Theatre from the disaster which threatens it — not, I repeat, from outside, but from within. For these workers know well that they are interdependent. If they could only agree upon a common language, they would find that language based upon their responsibility to, their love and respect for, and their belief in the Theatre, for which they work and by which they would soonest live.

IT has been a strange feeling reliving in my mind these thirty-three years. I have looked at my life quite impersonally, as though I were watching someone else. It has been an interesting existence, it seems to me. There is much to be grateful for. First of all I started with a definite purpose, and that is always an advantage. I have been tremendously lucky, even in misfortune ; I have had some hard knocks but usually deserved them ; on the whole I have been outrageously spoiled and have enjoyed it immensely !

So much for the past.

Now what of the future ?

Has my dream of a Civic Repertory Theatre come to an end ? For the moment, under present conditions, the answer must, I suppose, be "Yes." For the future I emphatically refuse to make the answer anything but "No !"

When I first started the Civic Repertory Theatre, I looked upon it as a beginning towards a far greater end.

My complete dream was this:

That there should be in New York City a large Centre

comprising two repertory theatres ; one large (say 3500 seats), the other intimate (possibly 1000).

In the large theatre a great variety of productions on a big scale, including opera and operetta. The intimate theatre to be used for plays classic and modern, American and international, conventional and experimental.

Both theatres to be run at popular prices.

A free school directly connected with these theatres.

A library on all branches of art.

An art gallery where young and unknown artists of talent might exhibit free of charge and where interesting exhibits of all kinds might be arranged.

It seemed to me that such a Centre would be of immense importance and would find great response from the people of New York.

This I still firmly believe.

I do not believe in spending millions in vast buildings holding nothing. We are too familiar in New York with such purposeless White Elephants.

In Miss Glaspell's play "Inheritors" Professor Holden says : "You say, 'Enlarge that we may grow.' That's false. It isn't of the nature of growth."

I wanted to do it the other way.

As soon as the Civic Repertory Theatre seemed to have established itself even in a small way as something of importance to the public, I added a free school and then a library ; all small, perhaps, but useful, and capable of strong healthy growth which might then have led to enlargement.

It still may.   It is still there.   It is ready.

So much money is spent lavishly, without aim, economy, or wisdom.

In the meantime I shall wait, I shall work, I shall learn.

I feel like saying with Silas Morton of "Inheritors" : "We're not old.   Let's fight !"

It may be that others will achieve the thing of which I have dreamed.   That doesn't matter as long as the dream materializes.

If the New York Civic Repertory Theatre proves to be the pioneer that has prepared the way for such a condition, I shall feel that its work has not been in vain.

And finally, when I've worked long enough and my services are no longer needed, I intend to fulfill the greatest of all my dreams : To live in the country, surrounded by trees, flowers and "millions and millions" of animals, and "millions and millions" of books ; then like Alice in "Through the Looking Glass" I shall have reached the final "Square" in this funny old chess-game we call "Life."

APPENDIX

APPENDIX

THE term Repertory has been used often in this book; let us have a look at this poor misused word and settle its *true* meaning. It is becoming almost as battered through mishandling as those old veterans "love" and "genius" ! I will let Granville Barker speak. There could be no better authority.

"A repertory theatre, according to the enthusiasts, may be anything from the Comédie Française to a band of beginners who produce plays haphazard in a back drawing-room and are animated by what they call the repertory idea. What, in heaven's name, is that ? You might as well have an idea that you run a motor-car by pouring petrol in somewhere — into the radiator, perhaps. If the term 'repertory' is to keep any specific meaning at all it should only be used for an organization by which plays are kept as ready for the stage — to make comparison between a simple and complex business — as books are kept to your hand in a library. If a clearer definition is needed — and if one is to argue the advantage of a system one cannot be too clear — it will be found that, as a matter of practice, the 'repertory idea' must consent to be bound by conditions very near akin to the following. In the theatre expressing it no single play must be given for more than two or three performances running, or for more than three or four in a week, and at least three or four different plays must be performed in a week ; so that as a consequence no one play can be performed more than about a hundred times a season. But it may be played in every one of a hundred seasons, as, no doubt, certain plays in the repertory of the Théâtre Française have been. And a theatre is not worked in this way because of some vague ideal behind it, but because the demand it thus fulfills involves this particular sort of organization, and can be satisfied by no other — as is demonstrable and as we had better proceed to demonstrate.

"A 'stock' theatre, with a permanent company producing fresh plays week by week, or month by month, is not a repertory theatre. A permanent company is in itself a very desirable thing ; but to produce a play at one time, let it lapse, and revive it at another is no more to keep it alive than it would be if the process were applied to a human body. Nor, again, is a season of a few months or less, in which half a dozen plays — for all that they are played variously week by week — have been rehearsed at a stretch by a company especially engaged for them, more than by courtesy a repertory season. It is at best a temporary lath-and-plaster façade for a repertory theatre. Walk up the steps, push open the door, and there is nothing behind. There are, moreover — it may be stated pretty dogmatically — only two logical and economical ways of organizing the drama as a continuing and professional activity : by a full-fledged repertory system, if artistic economy is what you are after ; for long runs, if you want to take all the money you can in the shortest possible time (you may equally lose it). *All compromise between the two systems means waste of money or of energy, extravagance and treble the work for half the result — not even for half, indeed, but rather for a different kind of reason altogether.*"

CIVIC REPERTORY RECORD
1926–1932

Plays	Authors	Opening Date	Number of performances given in the six seasons
1. Saturday Night	Benavente	October 25, 1926	14
2. The Three Sisters	Tchekov	October 26, 1926	63
3. The Master Builder	Ibsen	November 1, 1926	56
4. John Gabriel Borkman	Ibsen	November 9, 1926	28
5. La Locandiera	Goldoni	November 22, 1926	55
6. Twelfth Night	Shakespeare	December 20, 1926	39
7. The Cradle Song	Sierra	January 24, 1927	164
8. Inheritors	Glaspell	March 7, 1927	33
9. The Good Hope	Heijermans	October 18, 1927	60
10. 2 × 2 = 5	Wied	November 28, 1927	16
11. The First Stone	Ferris	January 13, 1928	20
12. Improvisations in June	Mohr	February 26, 1928	17
13. Hedda Gabler	Ibsen	March 26, 1928	34
14. The Would-be Gentleman	Molière	October 1, 1928	51
15. L'Invitation au Voyage	Bernard	October 4, 1928	20
16. The Cherry Orchard	Tchekov	October 15, 1928	108
17. Peter Pan	Barrie	November 26, 1928	129
18. The Lady from Alfaqueque	Quintero	January 14, 1929	35
19. On the High Road	Tchekov	January 14, 1929	18
20. Katerina	Andreyev	February 25, 1929	19
21. The Sea Gull	Tchekov	September 16, 1929	64
22. Mademoiselle Bourrat	Anet	October 7, 1929	25
23. The Living Corpse	Tolstoi	December 6, 1929	35
24. The Women Have Their Way	The Quinteros	January 27, 1930	38
25. The Open Door	Sutro	January 27, 1930	26
26. A Sunny Morning	The Quinteros	April 7, 1930	13

Plays	Authors	Opening Date	Number of performances given in the six seasons
27. Romeo and Juliet	Shakespeare	April 21, 1930	60
28. The Green Cockatoo	Schnitzler	October 9, 1930	9
29. Siegfried	Giraudoux	October 20, 1930	23
30. Alison's House	Glaspell	December 1, 1930	27
31. Camille	Dumas	January 26, 1931	91
32. Liliom	Molnar	September 24, 1932	53
33. Dear Jane	Hinkley	November 14, 1932	11
34. Alice in Wonderland	Carroll	December 10, 1932	127

Total number of performances in six seasons 1581